TO:

_____

FROM:

_____

DATE:

_____

Healing

FOR
THE
HOPEFUL
HEART

True Stories of
God's Mysterious Ways

DaySpring

LIVE YOUR FAITH

Healing for the Hopeful Heart: True Stories of God's Mysterious Ways
Copyright © DaySpring Cards, Inc. All rights reserved.
First Edition, November 2020

Published by:

21154 Highway 16 East
Siloam Springs, AR 72761
dayspring.com

Scriptures quotations marked NIV are taken from the Holy Bible, New International Version®, NIV®. Copyright © 1973, 1978, 1984, 2011 by Biblica, Inc.® Used by permission of Zondervan. All rights reserved worldwide. www.zondervan.com. The "NIV" and "New International Version" are trademarks registered in the United States Patent and Trademark Office by Biblica, Inc.®

Scripture quotations marked NLT are taken from the Holy Bible, New Living Translation, copyright © 1996, 2004, 2007 by Tyndale House Foundation. Used by permission of Tyndale House Publishers, Inc., Carol Stream, Illinois 60188. All rights reserved.

Scripture quotations marked THE MESSAGE are taken from THE MESSAGE, copyright © 1993, 1994, 1995, 1996, 2000, 2001, 2002 by Eugene H. Peterson. Used by permission of NavPress. All rights reserved. Represented by Tyndale House Publishers, Inc.

Scripture quotations marked KJV are taken from the Holy Bible, King James Version.

Produced with the assistance of Peachtree Publishing Services
Cover Design: Greg Jackson at Thinkpen.Design

Printed in China
Prime: J2434
ISBN: 978-1-64454-813-4

Contents

Introduction

You hold in your hands a very special book—a book full of true stories told by the people who lived them. More than anything, we want this book to encourage your heart and fill you with hope—hope that no matter what you're facing, God is right there with you. He's with you in the middle of the pain, the heartbreak, and the unknown.

As you'll see in these pages, sometimes God shows up in big ways, and other times He shows up in unexpected ways. You'll also see that God doesn't always answer our prayers in the way we prefer, but He's always there to walk with us through every circumstance. Some of these stories have happy endings, but some don't. Nevertheless, what connects these stories is the hope that no matter what, "we know that in all things God works for the good of those who love Him, who have been called according to His purpose" (Romans 8:28 NIV).

Undoubtedly, we will experience tragedies and trouble in this life, and perhaps we will never understand why God allowed such pain and heartache. But what we *can* hold on to is the hope that He's walking with us as He works everything out for our good and His glory.

From Desperate to Hopeful

Roy's Story

In 1950, at the age of forty, my dad was a broken man. His business had failed, his health had failed, and his marriage was failing. He was looking at certain divorce and the reality of losing custody of his two sons. That thought, along with everything else that was caving in around him, drove him to despair. He had decided he would take the lives of his family and then end his own life. Oddly enough, in the midst of all that turmoil, he decided he would go to Las Vegas for "one last fling" and then come back to LA and end it all.

"You don't belong here, Joe," spoke an unfamiliar voice. Startled, my dad quickly turned to see who was speaking to him. The gambling casino was crowded with people, but no one was within speaking distance. Puzzled, he tried to turn his interest back to the gambling tables, but he soon lost interest and decided to return to his hotel room.

Maybe I'll write something, he thought, but as he looked around the room, he couldn't find any paper to write on.

Maybe I'll read. Again, there was nothing in sight. He started opening some of the dresser drawers and once again came up empty. In one final attempt to find something to occupy his thoughts, he opened the drawer in the nightstand. His eyes instantly fell upon a book. Curious, he picked it up and looked at the cover. "A Bible!" he exclaimed.

My dad, who was raised an orthodox Jew and spent years in the synagogue, had never seen an English Bible. Curious, he turned to the book of Genesis, sat down, and started to read. The hours flew by as he read late into the night.

The next day, he decided to check out of his room and return to LA. His plan to destroy his family was put on hold. Not knowing where he could get another Bible, he decided to steal the one from his room. He packed his clothes in his suitcase, where he also put the Gideon Bible along with an ashtray and a towel, which he also stole from the hotel. When he returned home, he hid the Bible. He kept it under the bed and secretly read it whenever he had the chance.

A few months passed, and while he was reading in the book of Isaiah, he came across the following passage: "For unto us a child is born, unto us a son is given: and the government shall be upon His shoulder: and His name shall be called Wonderful, Counsellor, The mighty God, The everlasting Father, The Prince of Peace. Of the increase of His government and peace there shall be no end, upon the throne of David, and upon His kingdom, to order it, and to establish it with judgment and with justice from henceforth even for ever. The zeal of the LORD of hosts will perform this" (Isaiah 9:6–7 KJV).

My dad's eyes were opened. He knew that Jesus was the One the prophet spoke of, the One who was his Savior. He fell to his knees and prayed, confessing that Jesus was his Messiah and asking God to save him. From that point on, my dad radically changed. His fear of death vanished, peace entered his spirit, and hope was born in his heart.

When the Gideon organization heard how one of their Bibles, stolen from a Las Vegas hotel room, had been used by God to help bring a Jewish man to a personal faith in Jesus Christ, they invited my dad to share his story at various Gideon gatherings. That led to his story being written in their national magazine and an invitation to speak at their International Convention in 1960. At the request of my dad, I attended the convention as a young college student, and it wasn't until years later that I realized God used this event in His strategic plan to bring me to Jesus.

In the year 2000 my dad was diagnosed with leukemia and told he had a short time to live. He was eighty-nine. When he heard the news, he excitedly exclaimed, "You mean in a few days I will get to see the Lord!" He couldn't wait. When people came to visit him, my dad would say,

"Before you leave, let me give you my new mailing address."

When he passed, most of his children were present. Instead of sadness, joy filled the room. We all knew how much he wanted to be with Jesus, and we couldn't help but celebrate his heavenly homecoming.

—adapted from *Like Those Who Dream* by Roy Lessin, cofounder of DaySpring Cards, Inc.

BE ENCOURAGED: In your darkest moments when you are lost, hopeless, or discouraged, remember that God is your one Source of hope, peace, and healing.

When Life Throws Tough Pitches

Brian's Story

Growing up in Kentucky and playing baseball morning, noon, and night, I had strikes called against me and would still connect on the next pitch for a hit. When I was twenty-four years old, as a result of a lot of hard work and training, I was prepared to help the New York Yankees win the 1978 World Series when *The Call* came. Playing all six games—batting .438 with seven hits (including a double and two RBIs) and scoring four runs—was a dream of a lifetime! The month after the 1978 World Series, I cofounded the Doyle Baseball School along with my two brothers, Denny and Blake. Our desire was to help young people excel in the game, and that's what we set out to do. Work at the baseball school filled my professional life for twenty-five years.

Life threw me and my wife, Connie, a series of tough pitches when I was forty years old. First, a doctor told me at the Moffitt Cancer Center that I had hairy cell leukemia (HCL)—*strike one*. Pressed for further information, the doctor gave me just six months to live—*strike two*.

My response in the exam room was quick—nearly as quick as my lightning-fast reactions on the infield. Grabbing the doctor's shoulders, I exclaimed, "I don't know you, and you don't know me. I have one question for you: Are you here to win?"

The startled physician answered, "Yes!"

I replied, "When do we start?"

The innovative cancer treatment (invented by my physician) brought on bouts of nausea. On a particularly rough day, I implored God for help and read this passage from the apostle Paul: "Praise be to the God and Father of our Lord Jesus Christ, the Father of compassion and the God of all comfort, who comforts us in all our troubles, so that we can comfort those in any trouble with the comfort we ourselves receive from God" (II Corinthians 1:3–4 NIV).

A few moments later my twin brother, Blake, scooped me up in his arms and carried me to a chair placed at the open front door of my house. There, praying for me on our front yard, were members of First Baptist Church of Winter Haven, Florida. God had given me His words in Scripture only minutes before He physically showed me the meaning.

"It ain't over till it's over," one of my Yankee coaches, Yogi Berra, had famously said. This hit home with me when God answered His people's prayers and cured me of cancer. I was cancer-free!

In response to God's work of healing in my life, I quickly took up writing and giving chapel messages at our baseball school again. Years after that, I voiced to pastor friends what I'd felt inside for some time—a call to enter the ministry. Every pastor that I spoke to said, "It's about time you were obedient."

When I was fifty years old, I interviewed in front of a large group of pastors. I was grilled on theology and knowledge of the Scriptures. Finally, they gave me approval for ordination. Fifty years old—the Year of Jubilee! I felt in my heart that God's leading was to give my share of Doyle Baseball School to my brothers. I walked into the house and said to Connie, "Well, are you ready to go to Alaska, Minnesota, Wyoming, or anyplace God tells us to go?" With her answer of yes, we prayed together. An opportunity came and resulted in eight joy-filled years in Fort Lauderdale, Florida, where I served as Pastor of Evangelism and Pastoral Care at First Baptist Church. The senior pastor was Dr. Larry Thompson, who had encouraged me years earlier to consider full-time ministry. I had shrugged off the idea. My all-consuming ambition at that time was the baseball school.

In late 2011, after my wife and I had moved to Georgia to be close to our adult children and grandchildren, I joined my old friend, Jeff Siegel, in the ministry he founded, Global Baseball. Jeff was once an instructor at the Doyle Baseball School, and we remained friends. Connie and I supported him in missions for years. What a perfect time of life to become a missionary! The ministry has grown and has a new name to match the growth—<u>Global Sports Federation</u>.

I no longer travel; even moving about the house is difficult with my newest diagnosis, Parkinson's disease. I also suffer from central pain syndrome, which is an acute bone pain. Yet my job isn't finished. I continue to train people who want to be involved in sports as an avenue to reach people with the truth about Jesus. A group of men from our church meet with me weekly for Bible study, prayer, and discipleship training. I also serve as the pastor to our missionaries. The Lord has surrounded me with a wonderful family who is always there when I call, full of love and support.

—Brian Doyle, Georgia, 1978 World Series Champion

Learn more about Global Sports Federation at <u>www.goglobalsports.org</u>.

BE ENCOURAGED: <u>We have a choice with every trial—to have a pity party or use the pain as a platform.</u> <u>Allow God to use the circumstances in your life as a platform to share with others God's grace and love through Jesus Christ.</u>

Our Sweet Miracle

Robin's Story

My first pregnancy went beautifully, so my husband and I expected a similar experience with our second. We opted for an all-natural birth at a midwifery center. All seemed to be going so perfectly. We even traveled out of the country to see family.

Upon our return, the midwife set up a routine anatomy scan a bit early. We wondered why, but it turned out that God had something in mind. We were excited to see our baby and didn't expect a single problem. However, three hours into the sonogram, we began wondering what might be wrong. We thought it could have been due to a new sonogram technician, but we had no way of knowing. The test results were not good.

My cervix was effaced 100 percent (cervix paper thin and labor just ahead) for no known reason. I was put on immediate bed rest. This was later changed to moderate rest because doctors believed nothing more could be done. We were told we would lose the baby, with no chance for hope. Thus began our tour of doctors, as we attempted to find anyone who could help us. Almost every doctor we consulted said the exact same thing: "You need to prepare to lose your baby."

One physician offered to try something, which at the time seemed slightly more promising than all other alternatives. We attempted to keep the cervix closed with a pessary (a vaginal insert) and scheduled a follow-up appointment. Upon checking back, another ultrasound revealed that not only was I completely effaced, but I had dilated enough that the baby could put her foot outside the womb. Physicians immediately hospitalized me in preparation to lose the baby. Again they asked if we wanted to terminate the pregnancy, but we said no.

We felt blessed beyond measure that a friend had a miracle baby and could recommend an excellent hospital to us. We asked for my immediate transfer to that facility, where we found the doctors extremely encouraging. They even agreed to admit me before the official gestation marker for viability.

After the rupture had become infected, the doctors determined that in order to save both me and the baby, it was time for Eliora to be born. So it was that on June 27, 2017, at 11:15 p.m., Ellie was born at twenty-one weeks and six days of gestation. Weighing 13.6 ounces, she was just under 10.5 inches long.

Even for the hospital where she was born, this was extremely early. The health professionals there had established twenty-two-week gestations as their earliest births, but Eliora came in just under that threshold. The staff told us again and again that she was unlikely to be born alive, but from the moment she was born, she began to defy the odds.

Right after her birth, Eliora was pink and swinging her impossibly tiny arms and legs. The medical staff took her to be intubated, and this procedure (to assist with breathing) involved some risks. However, the tube went in, and immediately her chances of survival rose.

After that, she seemed to be settling into life extremely well in the neonatal intensive care unit (NICU). Ten days into the stay she once again scared us by falling into hypovolemic shock (a condition that results with loss of more than 20 percent of one's body fluid). Again, the physicians were certain that we'd lose her, but we gathered our church congregation behind us and prayed. Once again, Eliora pulled through with flying colors.

During Eliora's NICU stay we heard mentions of possible conditions such as cerebral palsy, bronchopulmonary dysplasia (this can come about in newborns as a result of mechanical ventilation), and intraventricular hemorrhage. We listened to health professionals tell us about possible severe mental disability and blindness, plus the likelihood that our daughter would be unable to carry out basic functions like breathing, eating, walking, and talking on her own. We also were warned of potentials such as a severely damaged immune system, asthma, and low quality of life.

Eliora has *none* of these things. Other than some minor lung issues and learning delays, she is the most perfect walking, talking, brilliant, hopeful, loving, scintillating child you will ever meet. God took one of the most insecure and unhopeful pregnancies known and brought out one of the brightest gems in our lives.

—Robin Schneider, Missouri

BE ENCOURAGED: God knows us while we are yet in the womb. It is by His hand that we are knit together. We are born for purposes of His design.

Jesus Redeemed My Painful Past

Anonymous

My freshman year of college held out hope. Moving to another part of the state, I thought I could leave my past behind. But life doesn't always work that way. Even in leaving, I was afraid for my family. I didn't think they'd survive. I recall having vivid dreams in which I'd learn that my father or my brother had died. At home I had been the buffer during their arguments.

We were a sad, scared mess. My father's drinking had escalated in the year before, even as my mother's depression deepened. My brother ran away repeatedly. In midsummer the situation exploded and I left home to escape. By the time classes began, I was already using drugs as a way of coping with life. Numbness felt much better, so I took whatever drug was available.

Altered perceptions, however, do not change reality and its consequences. During one drug-induced experience, I was sexually assaulted. In October I received positive results on a pregnancy test, and the college infirmary made an appointment for an abortion.

At the abortion facility I knew that what I was about to do was so much more terrible than what I had endured. Still, I went through with it; I had an abortion. The months afterward were a blur. I think Jesus, in His mercy, allows our memories to fog at times to spare us.

In January I began a college class called The Bible as Literature. I hoped it would offer me some help, but truth be told, our professor never opened the Scriptures. God, however, had placed Christians in this class, and though I didn't know it, they prayed for me. It must have been obvious that I was troubled. They were patient, treating me as though I belonged with them. One evening I went with them to a concert. It was there that Jesus opened my eyes and came into my life. My need for a Savior was overwhelming, and Jesus enveloped me in love. I was so grateful to Him for so much relief and joy—so much that I could not sleep that night or all the next day.

It was, however, difficult to relax and trust Him. Difficult home life experiences make it hard to develop trust. Families like mine, affected by alcohol and depression, are often subject to change. After drunken arguments, for example, aunts, uncles, cousins, and friends may disappear for years. Music may be enjoyed one night and the stereo smashed on the floor the next. Healthy boundaries are crossed, lies are told, and no one feels safe. While it may be natural for many children to trust their parents, I did not find trusting to be easy.

Faithful and patient, Jesus did not reject me because I was slow to completely trust Him, to believe that there is no "subject to change" in Him. Confidence in His wisdom and love for me came with time. I no longer had only my own resources to cope with problems. I was not alone. He was and is with me and in me.

God works in all things for our good—not just the positive experiences or isolated events, but in *all* things. When Jesus redeemed my past, He began to transform it into something that He could use for my good and for His glory.

Today Jesus allows me to come alongside teens. He gives me opportunities to encourage people with experiences similar to my own to trust Him. This also gives me an opportunity to reflect on my teen years but now with hope and joy. The children of unstable homes ravaged by alcohol abuse are expected to suffer in similar ways during adulthood—broken relationships, depression, failed marriages, abuse. In Jesus, however, a pattern is broken. I am so grateful to Him for the loving husband and children that He has given me, as well as for the work He has given me to do and for the body of believers He has placed me in.

There is never regret in trusting Jesus. His promises are true. Whatever our story is, He is able to redeem it and bring peace, joy, and hope. He has given me forgiveness, a wonderful life, and assurance of living in His presence forever.

—Anonymous

> **BE ENCOURAGED:** God does not change or disappoint. He is ever faithful.

Healing in God's Time and in God's Way

Jodi's Story

At times with the basketball in play, my adopted son Kayden would simply stop and stand on the court for a few seconds before continuing. These episodes were described to me as absent seizures—different from those that convulse the victim. A stutterer at age two, Kayden had an electro-encephalogram (EEG) a year later. I was told that a "blip" showed up. Two possibilities were outlined—either a hereditary marker or an indication of seizures. If further symptoms show up, he should be brought back for more testing.

Periods of exhaustion followed for Kayden. There were times when someone would be talking to him, but he wouldn't answer and would act kind of funny—like a toy running out of battery. Magnetic resonance imaging (MRI) helped physicians to pinpoint the absent seizures. They started Kayden on medication, then changed his regimen as they tried to deal with his adverse reactions. Some drugs didn't help, even as their dosages increased.

During the next few years Kayden struggled in school, where he'd sometimes fall asleep in classes. He also experienced bedwetting—possibly related to his illness or the medication. The seizures were seemingly controlling his life. As a single mom, it was difficult for me to constantly watch him, even while he was swimming, riding bike, anything! Each night Kayden, his older brother, Raymond, and I prayed for healing, and every day brought new challenges. I told the daycare workers that if a seizure exceeded five minutes, they must call 911.

One undesirable side effect of medications was vomiting. Because Kayden would often get sick, we couldn't always do fun things we had planned. For example, we had to cancel a family camping trip one weekend after he threw up in the car.

Kayden struggled to connect with his classmates. He felt insecure because he would black out randomly, and afterward he wouldn't know what the other kids were talking about. Initially, I didn't allow Kayden to play sports and risk complications—I didn't know whether the seizures were hereditary or if he had suffered a brain injury due to abuse before adoption. I eventually relented, however, and signed him up for basketball.

A very low point for our family occurred after Kayden seized in the car as we left a healing crusade in Lansing, Michigan, where people had prayed for him. And yet I found strength and resolve welling up inside and told him, "Kayden, we're not taking this. I know that you're going to get healed, and we're not giving up. We *are* going to trust God, and He *will* heal you." Knowing that God would heal him in His time and in His way, I persisted even when Kayden no longer wanted others to pray for him.

At our church one Sunday, a missionary told a story about a boy at his church in Germany who received healing after people had prayed for him. As we stood in the foyer after the service, the missionary shared with Kayden some verses from the Bible and prayed for him. It was a very holy moment; everything slowed down, but there were no goosebumps or anything like that.

Anticipating another EEG appointment, I noticed something and checked with teachers and daycare workers. No one could remember Kayden's last attack. I realized that his last seizure had happened before the missionary prayed for him. The EEG workers used their methods (sleep deprivation, strobe light upon waking) to help instigate an observable seizure, but Kayden didn't seize. Afterward they questioned Kayden, with me responding that my son had been healed after he'd been prayed for at church. "That's awesome!" the nurses replied.

Test results later showed a clean EEG and revealed no abnormalities. "This is it!" I cried jubilantly when I received the test results. "This is the proof." I looked for Kayden to tell him the good news and found him in the hallway.

"I was just thanking God so much for healing me," he told me.

At a subsequent doctor's appointment, I smiled the whole time and said, "There are no seizures."

With the clean EEG in hand, the physician asked many questions. Then he concluded, "Well, I don't know . . . okay." He agreed to slowly withdraw my son from medications. "I've never had a patient just stop having seizures in my entire career," the physician (who was in his seventies) told me.

"Well, you just did!" I replied.

—Jodi Casteel, Michigan

BE ENCOURAGED: God's healing ability knows no bounds. Trust Him. God's Word tells us that "the earnest prayer of a righteous person has great power and produces wonderful results" (James 5:16 NLT). This is truth we can stand on, even if we are on our knees.

In a Field of Flowers, I Laughed and Ran to Him

Ann's Story

Before I even knew God existed, He was with me through many difficult moments in my life until I became fully aware of His presence.

My dad, an alcoholic, was abusive to us before he and my mother separated. Mom worked hard making a home for us four children in three different towns in New York during my school years. I was eventually able to get a degree in business and became employed at the University of Rochester, where I worked, made friends, traveled, and met the man I later married. Then when our son Eric was born, I quit work to become a full-time mom.

Two other sons, Peter and Jason, followed. But I became concerned for our marriage. Without really knowing it, I was searching for the Lord. Now I see that. I began attending daily Mass as well as periodic inspirational lunches. At a Good Friday service, I heard the Lord telling me that He died for me. Stunned, I remained standing even as the whole congregation took their seats.

At a church luncheon, I remember hearing the lyrics "Reach out to Jesus, He is reaching out to you." My spirit was stirred—torn open, I would say—and the song pierced to the depths of my soul. Afraid, I ran for the ladies' room. Following me in, a lady named Jean asked if I wanted to accept Jesus as my Savior, and I did. I ran straight into the arms of Jesus, becoming His from that moment. His presence shook me to the marrow, and I experienced peace in my being. I desperately needed Him for what was happening in my life.

No matter what I did in my marriage, it didn't seem to be enough. I couldn't make my husband want to be with me. God held me throughout my divorce and the challenges of raising my boys. I read Psalm 51 every day for a month (it was suggested to me) and then started reading the Bible, beginning with Hebrews. I also attended Bible studies.

Our home's conflict and tensions were gone, but single parenting brought its own set of problems. I learned to manage the house, job, finances, and care of my sons. Crazy, unexpected things happened—replacing the car three times in one year, for example. No matter what, I learned to just move on and deal with issues as they arose.

When Eric was seventeen, he needed knee surgery. The anesthesia prompted his body to react in a condition called malignant hyperthermia. It manifests as a fast rise in body temperature and severe muscle contractions. The physicians figured out how to correct it. Later, Eric was hit by a car while biking and needed another surgery. Lacking words to pray, I just hugged my Bible. Eric came through that surgery too.

After years of knowing the Lord, however, I somehow got "stuck" and stopped attending church. But the Lord found a way. A friend had experienced dramatic change through a discipleship program called the Christ-Life Solution (CLS). I pushed off her suggestions that I deal with my old issues. Then, while visiting one of my sons, a roommate's father showed up—loud, obnoxious, and toting a big bottle of whiskey. Frightened, I ran and hid. "He reminds me of my father," I told my son. There it was. I needed to deal with past issues.

My healing began at my first CLS meeting. God was just waiting for me with love. I needed to release my pain and hurts to Him. As I did so, renewal swept over me and all my pieces came together. The empty spot was filled with His glorious presence.

After my sons all graduated from college and married, I decided to take piano lessons. The instructor encouraged us to be creative. So—in what was a one-time event—I wrote a song with these lyrics: *Run to Jesus; He knows your name.* God showed to me a picture of a little girl, laughing and running to Him in a field of flowers with her arms out-stretched. He was letting me know He was there with me through all my childhood. I was His before I knew Him.

—Ann Gottorff, New York

BE ENCOURAGED: <u>Run to Jesus</u> with any problem, whether big or small, and cling to Him. <u>Plod on</u>, even when you cannot see very far in front of you. <u>Trust</u> that He is with you in the fog, guiding you and strengthening you.

Learning to Trust My Provider

God is powerful to heal people from physical, emotional, and relational suffering. In my case, He wanted to heal and transform my old ways of thinking about money.

My years growing up were marked by what I refer to as an indoctrination in the "rules of the faith." Overwhelmingly, these rules address what a person *does* as a Christian rather than who a Christian *is*. To put it another way, I did not learn from my parents about God loving me simply because I was His. Instead, Christian duty was the central focus rather than acting from a motivation of love for God. When the church doors were open, I was there. When the plate was passed, I gave—simply because I thought I was supposed to. I felt that I "owed" the Lord.

Then during college, I met a girl who attended my church. We eventually were married. When she later became restless in that church, I initially resisted changing churches. But God helped me see that He had other plans for us. We left the denomination of our parents. Then through the faithful prayer of my wife and my pastor, the Lord saved me at the age of thirty-eight.

For the first time I recognized that the Lord loved me because He had made me, not because of what I could do for Him.

Several years later, we visited a church where we found people welcoming, and quickly we felt at home. One week, we were invited to a meeting attended by what appeared to be the solid members of the church. It turned out to be an initial meeting about a church expansion project—a building campaign for which financial commitments were needed.

Here we go, I thought. *They are after money!* Thought patterns from my upbringing kicked in—not just that I "owed" God; I also "owed" the church. What a person gave was linked with what that person got out of the church. For instance, I had grown accustomed to giving more for what I considered a good sermon or a touching service. Even after I'd developed a personal relationship with Christ, this thought pattern continued. Rather than giving out of thanks and love for God for His incredible gifts and blessings, my giving hinged on how well I felt the pastor had done.

So there we were, in a new church where they wanted a tithe—or 10 percent of our income—if not a substantial contribution to the building fund. "Even if you cannot give to the building campaign," the man leading the discussion had said, "at least begin to tithe." I left that meeting full of doubt and concern.

As I reflect on the next part of the story, I find it comical. The following morning was a Saturday in December. It began with snow and a temperature of seventeen degrees. I went to my office to rake the last of the leaves before they became buried under snow. Looking down at one point, I noticed paper money among the leaves. It turned out to be a fifty-dollar bill! Thinking at first it must be some kind of trick, I looked closely, then quickly stuffed it into my pocket. As I looked around for more, the Holy Spirit spoke to me and let me know that God is the Great Provider. Only the Lord knew where I would be raking. And He knew that five, ten, or twenty dollars would not have gotten my attention. But a fifty-dollar bill sure did!

As I returned to raking, I began to understand that giving isn't about paying for a service performed by the pastor. Instead, it is an act of trusting, loving, and worshipping the Lord. While I may have heard this in the past, I had never internalized it. I had never applied it to my own life.

I began to give a tithe to church that weekend. The prompting of the Holy Spirit began with my finances and was only the beginning of God's work of healing and transforming my heart and mind.

Worrying about finances had always been huge for me. But God is always completely faithful and trustworthy. I am grateful for His patience as I learn to listen to the Holy Spirit's promptings. With God smiling above, my thinking was transformed with a fifty-dollar bill in the leaves and snow.

—Bill McGough, New York

BE ENCOURAGED: Know that God is a generous Provider and can be trusted.

A Path to Healing

Daniel's Story

I can clearly look back at my life and see distinct catego-
ries of trauma I experienced growing up in a small town
in Oregon. Emotional and verbal abuse from my parents.
Homelessness when our house burned down. Depression,
anxiety, and passive suicidal ideation from chronic bullying.
Sexual abuse in high school and college from a pastor at my
home church. No wonder I showed up at the metaphorical
doorstep of college with a lot of baggage hanging off my arms.

My first night of college, a hot evening in San Diego
(it was probably normal weather for San Diego, and I, a
northerner, was just maladjusted), the reality sank in that I
was finally free—sort of. Though I was physically removed
from many of the people and situations that had harmed
me growing up, I distinctly remember going to a pastor at
the campus church and saying something along the lines
of "I just can't relate to these other freshmen complaining
about the pizza in the cafeteria when I'm trying to process
the last eighteen years of pain and confusion." Cue the genesis of my healing journey.

Currently, I'm smack-dab in the middle of my penulti-
mate semester of graduate school in counseling psychology,

and I work as a therapist in San Diego specializing in children and families. Praise God, the landscape of my life today—socially, emotionally, psychologically, and spiritually—is drastically different than it was even a few years ago. But how? What happened?

A brief rewind of my life, and you'll find that I was born into a complex family dynamic, riddled with generational trauma, avoidance, and overall unhealth. My mother was abused physically and emotionally by her alcoholic parents for twenty years. In her mid-adult life, she coped in many unhelpful ways: eating, sleeping, isolation, sudden and unpredictable outbursts of rage marked by throwing things at my sister and me, screaming, and hoarding—we kept every newspaper and soda can that ever entered our front door and owned thirty-seven cats despite the less-than-desirable square footage of our home and my debilitating allergies.

My mother also developed PTSD, claustrophobia, and intermittent explosive disorder. My clinical insight would consider her a likely candidate for borderline personality disorder. My father, stunned into silence and fear at my mother's psychological deterioration, avoided the family chaos by working multiple jobs, enabling my mother's habits, and reading the newspaper. At times he'd privately bandage us up (proverbially speaking) behind closed doors, but that gesture was often in vain when we were left exposed on the front lines to face our mom, as our dad rarely defended us in the heat of the moment. Needless to say, my parents didn't get along and our home wasn't fit for children.

In high school I began working at my church as the interim choral director for the worship department. Music has always been a healing balm for me, and it was a beautiful escape from our home environment. Fast forward to my senior year. I was couch surfing during this time, and the worship pastor invited me to live with his family in their guest room. A few months into this arrangement, and nightly sexual abuse became the norm. This persisted through half of my college career.

By my twenty-second birthday, I felt depleted of all resources, lacking bandwidth to handle any more curveballs from life. And then I happened upon Christians at my new church who embraced healing. *Real* healing. Juxtaposed to the rigid, harmful theology I was raised in that considered counseling an attempt at side-stepping Jesus, many of these believers were in therapy or were therapists themselves! There were literally fifteen therapists in this congregation. Some would call this a "God thing."

Pastors at this church financially provided means for me to undergo psychotherapy for anxiety and trauma, as well as treatment for the PTSD symptoms I'd developed myself. During this time, I received individual pastoral counseling and attended a weekly life group that led members in unpacking the lies we believed about ourselves as a by-product of our traumas.

Today, I'm thankful I no longer understand God to be an apathetic, bearded man in the sky, unconcerned with influential life events I had no control over. I now know God as the ultimate therapist. He is able to hold space for the entirety of my lived experience, emotions, thoughts, shortcomings, successes, and more. I know God to be radically accepting and embracing of all healing paths. And more than ever, God provides the consistency I previously never knew.

—Daniel Fuller, California

BE ENCOURAGED: Pain and shame have a way of convincing us that we aren't worth healing. But God says we're worth it. We can trust Him to place us on a path that leads toward healing.

God Heals the Hurting Heart

Brooke's Story

While on a family trip to Oklahoma to visit my stepson and attend my goddaughter's birthday party, I received a phone call from my oldest daughter, Meagan. She called to tell me she'd be heading to the lake with friends and would be away from her phone. "I love you," she said before hanging up.

Shortly after we arrived at the house, my ex-husband called me. He said that Meagan had been in a car wreck and was being transported by medevac to the Oklahoma University Medical Center. "Get there as soon as you can," he said. "It isn't looking good."

Soon we were off to the hospital—my youngest daughter, my mom, and me—in a forty-minute drive that felt like a six-hour trip. Rushing into the emergency room, my Italian-family background surfaced as I screamed, "My daughter was in a car wreck and I need to be with her!" When a chaplain approached, it seemed strange to me. He directed us to an area to await further word.

When I could wait no longer, I grabbed him by his shirt collar. "You better tell me what is going on," I demanded. Then I heard the words a parent *never* wants to hear: "I'm sorry, but your daughter was unable to survive her injuries."

"Tell me what is going on!" I yelled, not comprehending the words I had just heard. He stepped back and explained that Meagan had been killed by a drunk driver. Her body would become part of the evidence for felony charges against the driver. I couldn't hold her, kiss her, or tell her I loved her one last time.

I collapsed to the floor and begged God to take me instead. Eventually I realized I needed to let others know. First I phoned my husband, then our pastor, then others. I remember not wanting to leave the hospital because Meagan was there. I was sick—physically sick—but I stuffed my pain and tried to comfort those with me.

I felt an ache in my chest as we traveled back home to Missouri. Walking into our house, my emotional pain became excruciating. (It would take my youngest daughter three months before she could live at home instead of with a friend.) I selected clothes for burial and traveled back to Oklahoma. After the funeral, we buried Meagan next to her favorite set of grandparents.

As time crawled on, I learned how cruel the judicial system could be to victims. The other driver was granted bail. My sadness turned to anger and then to rage. Even as I continued going through the motions of living, I displayed aggression toward others. At bedtime, I'd start out in bed with my husband. But later, I'd find myself on Meagan's bedroom floor clutching her blankets and bawling. I pushed away my husband, who wanted to help me heal. A total wreck, I could not help my daughter, who slipped deeper into depression.

Every day at work, I quietly cried during my prekindergarten students' scheduled naptime. At my very lowest, the administrator called me in. Disagreeing with everything she said, I announced I was through, cursed, and slammed the door. I left the school and began walking home in below-zero weather without a coat. Eventually my husband responded to my call, came by, and picked me up.

I believed Satan's lie that I couldn't trust those whom I truly could trust—my husband, my friends, my church family. But God had a plan to break through to my heart. He used a wonderful woman—a stranger—who began a conversation with me via social media after I shared a post of hers. We never met face-to-face and are no longer in contact. It was literally God using someone to speak directly into my spirit to save me.

Through this woman's encouragement and the love of my heavenly Father, I could feel walls that I'd built begin to crack. Little by little over a period of years, I experienced healing in my broken heart, my marriage, and my relationships. To this day, I think how this strong woman of God had been obedient to Him and reached out to me. If she hadn't, I would likely be divorced and my youngest might even be dead. But this new friend spoke to me words of healing and hope as God came down to me in a way that He knew would get my attention.

—Brooke Howard, Missouri

> **BE ENCOURAGED:** God loved me enough to have a perfect stranger use social media to speak into the very depth of my heart and heal wounds. What He did for me, He can do for you as well.

Buried? Or Planted to Bloom?

Alyssa's Story

By all appearances I was thriving at age twenty-seven. I had an excellent job with good pay, a beautiful home, and many friends. My boyfriend was handsome. Excelling in all my fitness goals, I wore the most stylish clothes. In pursuit of my dreams, I never settled for anything less than what I deserved. An inspiration to people around me, I thought I had life figured out.

All this changed one summer afternoon when I was hurt badly by my boyfriend after he lashed out at me with some of the most defiling and angry words I had ever heard him speak. The words cut deep, reopening wounds of my past. I couldn't believe I had given someone my entire heart and all my trust, just to see him throw it all back in my face the second we had a little disagreement. After this, I resorted to old coping mechanisms—drinking alcohol, getting advice from the wrong people, and engaging in risky behaviors.

Hitting an all-time low, I was unfaithful to my boyfriend, thus completely losing his trust. Even worse, my infidelity was revealed to family and friends and blasted throughout our community and on social media. I could barely show my face in public. With the shame and guilt that I carried slowly killing me, I knew I needed help.

For the first time, I spoke to a pastor at my church, who encouraged me to start a Scripture-based program that focused on healing the "little girl" inside. Through it, I began accepting God's truths and practicing self-allying techniques to combat the lies I had told myself for years. During this process, I fully committed my life to Jesus and trusted Him to transform me from the inside out.

However, dedicating my life to Christ didn't exactly start out with a hallelujah. Within days, God began stripping away my worldly idols one by one. I lost my job, which had provided me not only my entire income but also my identity. I had already lost my boyfriend. Now it was my home, many of my friends, and my fit body. Soon, I possessed absolutely nothing of the things that I had dreamed of and planned out so carefully.

God stripped every last piece of me that held my identity and purpose. I was left down on my knees, at the foot of the cross, saying, "Take it; take everything I have. It always has been and always will be rightfully yours." After that, all I had was raw material—a crazy faith that Christ would somehow redeem my life and that He was using all of this for my good.

The next nine months brought even more pain and suffering, marked by a desperate search for my purpose in life. Unemployed, I was able to study the Bible, which became vibrant and full of color. It was no longer just a bunch of books. I got to know God on an even more personal level. He allowed me to rest in Him, listen, and just be still.

I established healthy Christian friendships and found a more affordable place to live. I began an amazing job in a Christian environment where I could reach out to dozens of people every day. I now use my God-given talents of music and leadership to give back to my church, and not to gratify myself. I am now a loyal disciple and follower of Jesus Christ. I surrender my entire life to the One who has better plans for me than any I could have made on my own.

Looking back, I realize that I was given the opportunity to rebuild my entire "house." Not everybody gets the opportunity to reorient their life when they accept Christ, but I did. Only months before, I thought I was being buried, but it turns out that Christ was actually planting me to bloom into the beautiful creation He had always planned for me to grow into.

He had it all figured out from the start. He provided. He protected. He sustained me. And now I thrive with Christ in a way I never would have before. God lit a fire in me. He sparked my passion for Jesus and for helping others combat lies with truth by putting Christ at the center of their lives. He radiates in everything I do. Through the dark days of suffering and pain, I received the very best blessing. Now I strive to live the way Christ lives and love the way He loves.

—Alyssa Smith, Minnesota

BE ENCOURAGED: We face this world's darkness on our own without a Savior. Don't wait to start a relationship with Jesus. Build now on a solid foundation by declaring that your life belongs to Him. Seek His kingdom first, because everything else crumbles in time.

With Us in Tragic Times

Kristy's Story

My world came crashing down with a phone call informing me that my husband had taken his own life. He had struggled with anxiety and depression, but never did I think that he would do this. Lying in bed that night, I wrestled with "What if?" and "What now?" Crying out, I asked God how I would ever raise four kids alone. My youngest had just turned two. Little did I know that God was already preparing my family's future.

My husband and I had realized—and prayed against—his struggle with anxiety, which was a generational issue and one we had observed in our oldest son. Then with his suicide, something rose up inside of me and demanded that this pattern end. As a healthcare professional, I knew the disheartening statistics related to children after a parent's suicide, but I reminded myself of the truth of God's promises found in the Bible.

In my mind, I saw myself standing over this "beast" of anxiety, my armor dented and bloodied. In one hand I held a sword and in the other, the beast's head. There would be no more compromise with the enemy. I publicly declared this at my husband's funeral, speaking words of life over those attending. In dark times that followed, God allowed me to walk through what Eugene Peterson refers to in *The Message* as God's "unforced rhythms of grace" (Matthew 11:28–30).

On the March afternoon of my husband's death, my oldest daughter had found him and called me. She was just eleven. How can a child recover from that? Many well-meaning people said that she'd require years of counseling and would have to relive that day to the point of becoming numb to it. However, my mom—who is a counselor—sat me down one evening. "That is not good enough for my granddaughter," she told me. So we began to pray and believe that God would heal her from this trauma.

Just days after the funeral, I noticed marker ink on my daughter's forearm. Calling her over, I looked at what she had written in permanent ink. There it was: "From God: I love you. Never give up on faith." She hasn't given up, and God has been so faithful to her. Later at a retreat, she felt Father God holding her and freeing her from all the mental images of her father's death.

As for me, I found that I could be a parent, make big decisions, buy a house, and take the kids on fun trips alone even when I didn't want to. I still struggled with loneliness. I wanted a partner to walk through life with me and continued to pray for that. About fourteen months after my husband's death, I received on social media a friend request from a man I did not know. Several people acquainted with my husband had already reached out to me in this way. When I asked the man if he had known my husband, he responded that he had been the medical examiner assigned to my husband's death. Though he couldn't explain it, our story had stuck with him. He wanted to be sure my daughter was doing okay. I messaged that we were all doing wonderfully, that God had been faithful to us, and that he really should meet the kids to put his mind at ease.

On a June afternoon, he brought his two little kids to my cousin's house for swimming and a cookout. He was different than anyone I had known before. During our talk about that day, I realized that at the very moment I was crying out to God that I didn't want to be alone, this man was hearing our names for the first time. He had already seen so many tragic things, yet our story stuck with him. I knew why: God had brought us together to be a couple. We were married fourteen months later. His calm, introverted personality is a perfect balance to my excitable, extroverted personality. He makes me see the world differently. God sent me a man who has the capacity to love another man's children as his own. My entire life I had wanted at least five children; I now have six! God was faithful to answer my cries to Him in ways that I could not have even imagined.

He sent me a wonderful man with a bonus of two additional children who fit perfectly within our family. Even amid the greatest tragedies and deepest sorrows, I know and have seen that God is good and His steadfast love endures forever.

Today my son is free of anxiety. As a successful husband and father, he lives unafraid. My oldest daughter was recently married and is working in our local church. God is so good.

—Kristy Calloway, Oklahoma

BE ENCOURAGED: God loves you. Never give up on faith in Him. Even amid trials, He has you in the palm of His hand.

From Ruined to Redeemed

After a troubled childhood, I enlisted in the military and was assigned to a special unit. After training, we were dispatched to a country near Vietnam. There, we wore only green fatigues, held no rank, and addressed one another by our last names. We weren't allowed any mail or communication to the outside.

Our orders were to maintain security for our base camp and all forward operating bases in the area. We would find out that this directive meant we'd be eliminating every living soul in any village within a one and three-fourths mile area of our bases.

In time, I found this task to be unethical, and three others shared my thoughts. Knowing the futility of trying to stop the madness, we went absent without leave (AWOL). About four and a half miles from base, we were ambushed by the Vietcong (VC), a communist guerrilla force that supported the North Vietnamese Army.

We were tortured, raped, and grilled for intelligence that the VC thought we had. Fortunately, we soon escaped but then were caught by our own Green Berets, who placed us on guard duty. Standing guard on the airfield, I was shot by a sniper and broke my neck.

Miraculously, and to the surgeon's amazement, I survived. As a hard-core atheist, I gave all the credit to the doctors and none to God. After my recovery, I was sent back home to the US to face judgment for going AWOL. After lengthy legal proceedings, to my surprise the military issued me an honorable discharge.

The first two years of civilian life were rough. I couldn't cope with the actions of my past. I turned to booze and cocaine to forget. Life was awful. Finally, sick of being sick, I decided to clean up my life. I put everything behind me, living as if I had never been to Southeast Asia. Nowadays, my psychiatrist tells me this was some sort of self-imposed amnesia. Rather than turning to substances to numb the pain, I threw myself into success in business. I married and held down some pretty impressive jobs.

Then—two decades afterward—it happened. Tragedy came to me due to problems with my business and my marriage. I started experiencing hallucinations, commonly known as flashbacks of war and torture. (These still happen to me today, although in most cases they are not as harsh as before.)

During this time, all that I had poured myself into fell apart and I returned to those methods of forgetting I had used in the first two years after I came home from war—drugs, alcohol, call girls, guns, and everything that comes with that life. As my life spiraled downward, I lost my wife and family. In a four-year period, I spent time in high-priced mental institutions and state-run facilities that were worse than jail.

My lowest point came in a maximum-security mental ward. In a straitjacket in a padded room, I was afraid for my life. Flashbacks and hallucinations took over me. I visualized a black tarlike substance coming out of my skin with terrible monsters surrounding me.

At first, I started cussing out God. Then, suddenly, in desperation, I cried out to God for help. Within a split second, everything stopped and I felt a calm come over me. I felt peace for the first time in longer than I could remember. Initially, I started thinking there was some scientific reason for this immediate relief. I then realized it was God intervening in my terrible life.

In that moment, I realized there was a God and that somehow, incredibly, in spite of my past and things I had done and had been done to me, God loved me! How could that be true? I knew I needed to find a church as soon as possible to find out the answer. I was confirmed and became a member of a local church, where I worshipped for about three years before moving to my current home church.

Through the community and teaching at those churches, Christ has brought healing I never believed was possible. I have a lot of catching up to do after being an atheist for so long. Nevertheless, I know I am on the right road now and Jesus Christ is transforming my terrible old life into something new by His amazing and gracious love.

—Anonymous

BE ENCOURAGED: God can take over and transform your ruined and wrecked life. <u>He can redeem anything and anyone</u>. His love covers a multitude of sins.

Searching for a Father's Love

Kayla's Story

Growing up without a father, I never knew what it was like to be loved by a dad. My mom had to work to provide for my two brothers and me, so I had little guidance, discipline, or love. By school age, I felt I never really fit in, even though I tried to get people to like me. Desperate for acceptance, I was never myself.

In high school, I lost my virginity, sleeping with boys for the comfort and love I always longed for from a man. To go to bed with them, however, I had to consume alcohol. From age fifteen on, I spent most weekends partying and drinking. Without structure in my life, I did whatever I wanted—all the while trying to fill the void of my absent father.

During those years, I smoked weed and tried cocaine and pills. There was nothing I wouldn't try. In my senior year, I dropped out of school and quit my job. I cared for nothing except having sex and getting drunk and high.

Not long after, I found myself married to someone I met after leaving school. We moved from where I had grown up. We mutually abused each other during marital fights, and I still drank all the time. When I had lost my job at a fast-food restaurant, my husband's friend suggested that I could become a stripper. His girlfriend was making good money at it. Why my husband didn't stop me from doing it, I don't know. I wondered if someone who loved me would allow it, but before I knew it, I was working my first night at a strip club.

To get through that first night I drank myself stupid. And I drank every single day to deal with my shame. Yes, I made good money, but I also used cocaine with my coworkers and my boss. When that lifestyle sent my husband packing, his departure only drew me further in.

At a club I was working, a pimp approached me with an offer. Initially I had no clue what he meant. When people tried to warn me, I didn't listen. A week later, a friend and I were at a hotel having sex with guys for money. To get through that, again I did drugs and drank.

In four years of prostitution, I was beaten up, used, and abused, and I fought back. I had two different pimps. After leaving the second one, I set about doing prostitution on my own. I even lured friends into doing this so that I wasn't working alone. I began using heroin and methamphetamines. My life was completely out of control.

No amount of money or drugs could heal the pain inside. When I finally called it quits on prostitution, I moved across the country to get away from that life. I thought of stripping as better than prostitution and began that again. I smoked methamphetamine regularly.

One night the girls I worked with injected me with something; I didn't know what it was. It put me in a mental hospital for a week. While there, I saw a bright light and I knew it was the Lord. I still carried in my mind the things my grandma had told me about God while I was growing up. But I had never experienced Him like this. I didn't think I could be forgiven, but He told me in His Word (the Bible) that He forgave me for everything I had ever done.

A couple of months after leaving the psychiatric ward, I successfully stopped using drugs. I finally got clean. Certainly, this wasn't by my own strength. The Lord pulled me out of that life and saved me.

I am redeemed. He loved me enough to save me. Now I live for Him. Though I still mess up at times, I am clean of drugs. My story has been passed around some, and this has allowed me opportunities to help others come out of the same lifestyle I endured.

Today I have a real job. I am married and have a son. God has been with me through this healing journey, and I am beyond thankful, grateful, and blessed. I found the love of a Father but not the father I was looking for.

—Kayla Hambly, Iowa

BE ENCOURAGED: <u>God loves us while we are still sinners</u>. He <u>reaches down</u> and <u>helps us look up</u> to Him.

God's Perfect Care

Megan's Story

We were thrilled to learn that I was pregnant with our second child and shared this news with close family and friends right after seeing the positive test results.

Into my second trimester, the pregnancy had gone very well, with great checkups. Then at nearly seventeen weeks, I was using the bathroom when my water broke. Shocked, I knew what was happening, and I cried out "Shalom!" which means "peace."

My husband, Lee, and I consider it a miracle that he was home for lunch that day. As he helped me, I phoned my midwife, who advised me about what to do and reminded me to talk with my dear friend Sabrina. Having been through a similar situation, Sabrina came right away to comfort and encourage Lee and me.

Relief accompanied the ultrasound technician's words: "There is a heartbeat, and the baby is alive." We were so thankful. My physician put me on strict bed rest to stop any contractions so that our baby would keep growing.

Within a mother's amniotic fluid during this period of gestation, a baby practices breathing. This is what strengthens the baby's lungs. I had little fluid left in my womb, so each day was a miracle. The breath of God was sustaining our little one.

Days became weeks and then weeks became months of bed rest—first at home and later at the hospital. My high-risk pregnancy was due to preterm premature rupture of membranes (PPROM), and my physicians could not offer much more than advice to wait until the baby comes.

In the stillness of those many quiet moments of bed rest, I got to know God like never before in my life. His voice became a whisper of love and comfort that I needed. A pregnant woman is often tallying numbers (weeks, months, trimesters, etc.), and I felt as if God was using numbers to express His love for me.

I had ultrasound after ultrasound, as Lee and I tried to find out whether we would have a boy or a girl. I will never forget the week we were about to give up on learning our baby's gender. Finally, on the ninth ultrasound we discovered that we would have a little girl. Some say the number nine means "being patient in His divine movement." It was just like God's sense of humor to let us know what little patience we had. Happy to know it was a girl, we named her Mirrah Kate, which means "a light and wonder of God" and "purity."

At twenty-eight weeks, I started having contractions as baby Mirrah wanted to be born. I ended up having an emergency C-section. She was delivered alive and crying, which was a wonder and miracle.

But while I was holding on to my life and recovering, Mirrah was fighting for hers like the warrior princess she was. Her lungs grew weaker and weaker and ended up collapsing after seven and a half hours of struggle. After she fell into Jesus' arms that day, I recovered—but not soon enough to meet my little Mirrah while she was still alive.

After all of this, God swept over my spirit with comfort and love. He revealed this to me: "Megan, do you realize that Mirrah Kate was born on the seventh day of September; she fell into My arms seven and a half hours later; and you buried her seven days after that?"

Awestruck, I told this to my friend, who shared my fascination. I was told that the number seven means wholeness, completion, and perfection. For me, I felt as if God was using it to bring me comfort as He walked me through this. God was using numbers to let me know that Mirrah was perfect and complete and that she was healed. After that special moment, I was one happy mommy.

When I shared this with Lee, he too was amazed. "I have more sevens to share," he replied. "All this happened in your seventh month of pregnancy, and we recently celebrated seven years of marriage." Our loving God covered our tragic situation with five sevens. Lee and I learned that

God is a very good Father, loving and caring in the midst of trials. God stayed with us through it all, offering peace, comfort, and a soft place to fall. And in His own magnificent way, He gave us the assurance of knowing that He was in control the entire time, and our Mirrah is complete and perfect and healed in His arms.

—Megan Troyer, Missouri

BE ENCOURAGED: God walks with us. He never abandons us to walk on alone. Look for the miraculous details. Listen for the Father's voice. He is there with you!

Beautiful, Harsh Lessons

Gabby's Story

S he is gone now. Even after a year, I still weep.

I think of Kyleigh when I go into her bedroom and when I smell the soap used during baths. Photographs elicit memories and I miss her.

She was brought to our home three days after her birth. After signing some papers, my husband, Daniel, and I became foster parents. Immediately she became ours—no different to us than if I had given birth to her. We bonded as if she were our own. We felt no need to protect ourselves emotionally or hold back on our love. Hopes and dreams for our future included Kyleigh.

The semiweekly visits with her birth mother, Faith, were logistically taxing and left us emotionally drained afterward. Then at our six-month court hearing, it became clear that Kyleigh would eventually leave our home to be reunited with her mom.

I don't know that Daniel and I have fully processed the days, weeks, and months that followed—or ever will for that matter. This season felt like waiting eight months (February to the following October) for the worst day of our lives. I say that, and yet I simultaneously experienced great sorrow and exuberant joy. God's instruction seemed to be that nothing and nobody is ever fully ours, and this would be the case even if Kyleigh were our biological child; she belongs to Him.

<u>God owes us nothing</u>—a lesson that I find beautifully harsh (if I can use those two terms together). Reflecting back, I am always brought to tears by what God taught us. <u>His love for us was manifested through our church</u>, community, and family, who brought, among other things, hot meals and diapers. We found listening ears in the people who sat in our home. What a gift. Daniel and I were finally able to arrive at a point at which Kyleigh's departure would be easier than having to anticipate her leaving.

Foster care is not something that can be wrapped up with a bow and delivered each week like a feel-good television show. Grief overwhelmed me, but the experience—unlike anything else I have been through—served as an impetus to place faith in the Lord. Maybe this was because God gave to me such a worthy task—that of loving a baby who needed it. In the midst of this hard lesson, I wanted to escape God's teaching. Now, I feel honored that He chose me to travel such a difficult and beautiful journey to begin to trust Him in ways I had not known were possible.

Since Kyleigh left our home for Faith's, we have seen her two to three times a month. We get to babysit her, take her to fun events, and at times, have her stay overnight. We get to see her grow—not just in height either. We have watched her increase in intelligence, develop her personality, and grow in maturity. All of these privileges are precious, but accompanying this joy is also a wound that opens over and over again. God continues to heal us through our relationship with Him, our trust in His promises, and the enjoyment of a new family we didn't expect: Kyleigh and Faith. While I find my times with Faith to be complex and at times difficult, I know that our relationship is also very important. God knew that I need to learn humility and how to better understand people less fortunate than I am. He's continuing to refine Daniel and me.

Our grief surfaced again when our son, Monty, was born. We wish that Kyleigh could be around our home as his big sister. This is at once extremely complicated and yet very simple. She remains, to us, our daughter and Monty's sister, and yet she is also someone else's daughter. When she first entered our home, we had little comprehension of how she'd change our lives and the lives of so many around us. We find in this an amazing picture of the gospel. God loved us so much that He lost a child so that we could fully lean on Him, even at a time when we lost ours.

—Gabby Kersey, Ohio

BE ENCOURAGED: One of the deepest, longest-lasting periods of grief comes with the loss of a child. <u>God can bring beauty and spiritual growth from anything</u>, but He often does so when we go through the difficulty and not when we shrink back from it.

Hurt Replaced by Joy

Jeni's Story

The day that Jeni* found work as a housekeeper for my friend Mushi put her on a good path toward significant healing in her life.

In addition to the housekeeping, the two had agreed upon an exchange: Jeni tutored Mushi in Swahili, and in return, Jeni learned from the Bible. Mushi helped her to become a follower of Jesus Christ. And yet, as time went on, Mushi concluded that the younger woman carried great sadness and anger inside.

Both of these Tanzanian women attended my seminar in which I outlined how we don't wrestle against flesh and blood. A spiritual enemy assails us, seeking to destroy our souls and bodies. I taught how we need God's healing and presence in our lives.

Weaving in stories from my family and ministry, I taught about the long-term impact of traumas. I gave the ladies the steps to freedom. My last topic was bitterness. After the seminar, Jeni revealed that terrible things had happened to her. "I have believed that God has forgotten me," she said. "I have been very bitter toward Him and others." Orphaned as a child, she had lived on the streets, scraping by on little more than a dollar a day.

I told the others that in extreme cases like Jeni's, a prayer for the Holy Spirit to bind up a broken heart is the first step to freedom in Christ. As they prayed silently, I put my hands on her shoulders and bowed my head. With empathy for this lovely, tortured girl, I began praying to the Lord. I spoke value over Jeni, announcing an end to years of neglect and harm. I could feel her shift beneath my hands, and I continued to pray while the other women in the room sang, "God is so good, He's so good to me." Then I asked for a second verse.

Slowly opening her eyes, Jeni looked around in confusion. I kept praying. Suddenly she shouted, "Oh! Oh!" and raised her hand, looking up and crying out, "Jesus! Jesus! Thank You. Thank You, Jesus!"

I had seen deliverance before, but I had not seen the Holy Spirit fill someone. "This is the Holy Spirit," I realized, amazed. He was filling her heart with His love.

As Jeni sobbed—a gut-wrenching release of pain and bitterness—I pulled her into my arms and spoke of the love of a father and mother. Then speaking as if I were her mother, I expressed love. I apologized for not having been there to give her hugs and comfort. I said that her heavenly Father would never leave and that He desires for her to be with Him forever.

I spoke of God's promise that the last will be first. She could go forward with new hope. I asked God again to reveal the depth of His love for her.

Jeni sat on her chair again. I went to mine, rather stunned. "How Great Thou Art" was led by a lady with a lovely voice, and we all sang loudly in a cappella. Jeni raised her hands, lifted her face, and in such grateful adoration sang every stanza. We sang another hymn, then prayed. After that, the ladies continued one hymn after another until the ride came for them.

When I gave Jeni some Scripture verses to memorize, she said, "I feel so free!" and contrasted it with earlier times of waking up with bitterness, anger, and fear. "Now I have this great joy in my heart."

—Missionary, Tanzania

Not the younger woman's real name

BE ENCOURAGED: Is anything holding you back from truly believing God loves you? The simple, profound truth of God's love for you should be allowed to wash over your soul and penetrate the depths of your heart.

A Mistake or a Miracle?

Jane's Story

My doctor came into the exam room, sat down, and said to me, "Well, dear, it's not good news. You have cancer." I wasn't expecting this at all when I had gone days earlier for my annual physical. Afterward, I received a call informing me that my Pap smear showed something wrong. I had the biopsy taken as advised.

Returning to the hospital alone, I repeated Scripture texts that I had memorized to quash any worries that came to my mind. I held out hope for healing. But the doctor gave me bad news.

"These are the treatment options," he said, handing me a packet. It was big and felt heavy. "You need to go home and decide with your husband which treatment you want to pick. Then give us a call so we can begin with it." He then patted my hand and left.

I lay there in the exam room for a long time, the thoughts racing through my mind. What would my death mean to my husband and to my mom and others? Everything around me seemed sterile, cold, and so white. I thought of dying. I thought that spending eternity in heaven would be wonderful—just not this soon.

"Well, Lord, what do You want me to do?" I said, looking upward. I seemed to hear Him say to me, "Throw the packet away; you are already healed." Still in my lovely white hospital gown, I got up to throw it away but not before peeking inside. I spied some brochures about treatment options, cancer centers, and support groups. It all went into the trash.

Arriving at home, I went right out to jump into our swimming pool. My regular routine was to first slather on sunscreen, then clean the pool of leaves, then stand beside the pool to read a passage from my Bible, and then get into the water and swim. On this day, however, I got in the water, opened my Bible (yes, reading in the pool), and prayed.

Almost immediately, I felt God all around me. As I attempted to figure out what was happening, I kept my eyes closed. His glory seemed to take me into a realm with no time. I'm not sure how long I stood in the water, but His power and presence were overwhelming. I sensed movement all around. Finally ratcheting up my courage to open my eyes, I peeked just a little and saw sparkles of every color raining down all around me.

"Lord, what is going on?" I asked. His answer was, "I'm healing you." Wow! What a time of praise and glory. When His powerful presence left, I decided not to tell anyone about the cancer because I had been healed.

That was on a Friday, and on the Sunday that followed, my husband, my mom, and I attended church services in the morning and again that evening. A small crowd showed up for the night service, where we hosted a missionary, a Russian man. After his message, our pastor went up front to ask the ushers to pass a plate for an offering for this Christian worker. The pastor was about to pray to dismiss us when he was interrupted.

"There is someone here who has just been diagnosed with cancer," the missionary said. "The Lord wants us to pray for you." As I slowly got up, I looked over at my husband and my mom. Both were in shock. I shrugged and walked to the front. "The Lord has already healed me," I told the missionary, who replied, "I know, but He just wants to confirm the healing to you."

Everyone gathered around me. We prayed, and I told them what had happened. Nobody had known about my diagnosis except for God and me, but how precious it is when the Holy Spirit works through another person to reassure someone. I never called the doctor back, but I received word weeks later that somehow a mistake had occurred at the hospital. I didn't have any cancer.

It wasn't a mistake; it was a miracle. I love how God had worked things out so I didn't even have to go back to the hospital to confirm my miracle. All the glory goes to my precious Savior, who healed me two thousand years ago by His suffering.

—Jane Rozier, Michigan

BE ENCOURAGED: Pray daily asking God to overwhelm you with His presence and His power.

Perfected for God's Purpose

Timothy's Story

As a nine-year-old, I witnessed the Lord's touch on my otherwise ordinary Irish Catholic family. At a weekend Marriage Encounter that my parents attended, a born-again priest led them in an authentic salvation prayer to receive Christ. Mom and Dad returned in love with each other and in love with Jesus.

Jesus became a new member of our family—in fact, the central figure. Rejoicing in my heart at what was happening, I too came to love Jesus. I experienced joy that I hadn't felt before.

About that time, I had been having a hearing problem. Two surgeries on my left ear had failed to produce results. Stirred by their newfound faith in Christ, my parents asked a local prayer group to pray for me. (Some of this group's members have become lifelong friends of mine.)

Seating me in a chair, these faithful people called upon Jesus concerning my ear. Within a week I began to notice a difference. I had grown so accustomed to saying "What?" that the phrase would come out automatically. However, I began to realize I could actually *hear* people.

Some days later at an appointment for my ear that had already been scheduled, I underwent a typical battery of hearing tests. It was similar to earlier tests but with something different. I was raising my left hand at least as much as the right, indicating that I heard the tones.

When I exited the soundproof room, the technician proceeded to tell my parents that my hearing was 100 percent. "In fact," he said, "his left ear is like that of a newborn baby. He still has the fine stereo cilia that kids usually lose at a young age, meaning he can still hear some high-pitch sounds that we can't."

"Wait, you don't understand," my parents said. "He has hearing loss in his left ear." It was news to the technician, though. And I never had the problem again. God had given me a brand-new ear.

Unfortunately, about this time, I began having periodic migraine headaches, which seemed to be triggered by the emotion of excitement. No pain medication or method worked. In intense pain, I sometimes banged my head against the bed headboard, trying to find some relief. I also suppressed emotions to try to avoid another headache.

The migraines lasted most of a day, leaving me too exhausted to attend classes or do anything. By age sixteen, the triggering came more easily, thus increasing in frequency. My family learned of an upcoming meeting with a Catholic priest who believed in healing.

At the conclusion of the meeting, the priest offered prayer for people in need of healing. When I approached him and told him about my migraine headaches, he reached out his hand toward my forehead to pray for me. However, before he could touch my head, I was overcome with something powerful and heavy.

I found myself lying on the floor. I immediately tried to get up but couldn't. As I lay there, I felt what I can only describe as waves of joy and peace flooding over me. On my next attempt to stand, an elderly lady got down on the floor with me. "Sonny," she said, placing her hand on my chest. "You just let the Lord do whatever He's doing."

After I eventually stood up, I never had a migraine headache again. Interestingly enough, when I was a senior in high school I applied for a Reserve Officer Training Corps (ROTC) scholarship in order to join the military as a commissioned officer. For a few years already, I had sensed a calling to become a military officer.

The scholarship requirements were intense, including physical exams and medical screening. Either the hearing issue or the migraine headaches would have disqualified me. Without the healings I could not have applied for any military training. Instead, I was offered full four-year

ROTC scholarships from the Air Force, the Army, and the Marines. I chose the Army.

In the ensuing years, I have been mobilized with the Army seven times, including a combat tour in Afghanistan. I served a twenty-five-year career, both in the Active Army and Army Reserves. The Lord healed me out of His compassion and because He knew the path He had for me.

—Timothy O'Brien, Missouri

> **BE ENCOURAGED:** Be ever alert to see what God has in mind for you. He will make it happen.

Beating the Odds

Sabrina's Story

I fearfully listened as the specialist presented my husband and me with a difficult choice: continue the pregnancy or abort our baby. We could continue my pregnancy, risking my life due to possible infection. And if I survived, complications from the pregnancy would potentially jeopardize my ability to have other children. The specialist highly encouraged abortion because she said even if our baby lived, he would have deformities and many medical conditions. She said other mothers made the decision to abort because it would give them a new start for a healthy pregnancy.

A couple of weeks earlier, I had received the midpregnancy sonogram at nineteen weeks. The results revealed that my amniotic fluid was not measurable and our baby was growing two to three weeks behind, meaning our baby would not be able to practice breathing and develop his lungs. The doctors referred me to a specialist.

When we first visited the specialist, she gave me instructions on how to potentially increase my fluid. I carefully followed the instructions, but after returning a week later, nothing changed. This was when the doctor outlined our options moving forward and told us there was nothing else we could do. After hearing the devastating report, we decided not to stop the healthy heartbeat of our child. My husband and I believe in God's power, specifically the power to heal. Though scientific facts told us our son would die, we held on to faith in God's promises.

We took the pregnancy one day at a time, believing God would protect my womb and sustain our son. At twenty-three weeks, I rushed to the ER, after more fluid loss, where I was given the diagnosis of PPROM (preterm premature rupture of membrane)—meaning my water broke. However, after discussions with doctors, it was determined that my water had broken six weeks earlier. Our son was diagnosed with IUGR (intrauterine growth restriction). For the next seven weeks, I was placed on hospital bed rest so doctors could closely monitor our baby and me. My husband and I, along with a community of prayer warriors, prayed that God would sustain our baby's life.

Initially, my doctors strongly warned that I would either catch an infection or go into labor within the week—but I didn't. We continued to prove the doctors wrong. When they said things would start to look worse, we saw things start to improve. God's healing hand was on my body.

A few days before our son's birth, he fully passed his biophysical profile for the very first time. God kept us not only stable but progressively thriving until the moment he needed to be born. God's timing is always perfect. At just over thirty weeks gestation our boy made his appearance during an emergency C-section. God orchestrated all the details and gave us the best surgical team. Our son, Truman, was born and immediately taken to the NICU (neonatal intensive care unit), where the doctors did some comprehensive testing, including X-rays. With complete shock, our doctors told us our son had more lung development than they expected. After birth it was determined the reason for his IUGR was because he hadn't received enough nutrients during the pregnancy. He had miraculously survived with very limited fluid and a severe lack of nutrition.

Truman's stay in the NICU was full of ups and downs, but thankfully he came home after ninety-seven days with no monitors or oxygen support. He didn't have any deformities, nor does he have any lifelong medical conditions. What God did for Truman is miraculous. We were told numerous times by nurses in the NICU that Truman was a miracle!

During his first year of life Truman was required to see specialists to ensure he was growing, but before his first birthday he was released from all programs and has continued to thrive. He is a happy, growing, very active little boy.

Truman was given little to no odds of survival, but with the help of God, he beat them. The doctors were adamant about the scientific facts. They weren't able to give us hope where medically there was none. We understood, but <u>we</u> <u>*knew* God was bigger.</u>

—Sabrina Schwindt, Missouri

BE ENCOURAGED: It is God who gives us the wisdom to use medicine and advanced medical technology. And it is God who sustains a baby's life in situations beyond the reach of what modern medicine can offer. <u>Science tells us the odds, but we know with the help of God we can "beat the odds."</u>

Cheering Me On

Anonymous

The musical *Bright Star* presents a powerful story of people who make serious mistakes, learn from their errors, and eventually find redemption, forgiveness, and hope. The message of "you're never too far gone to experience redemption and forgiveness" is woven throughout.

In the play, I was cast as Daddy Cane and as part of the ensemble—parts that come with a lot of singing and dancing. I also helped create and build the set for the production at Oral Roberts University (ORU).

At rehearsal, while doing a lift with a girl, things went really badly for me. I did something—I don't know what—to the hamstring of my left leg. I thought it was pulled, but later I wondered if the muscle might be cramping. I wasn't willing to go to the doctor, so people helped me by showing me some really good stretches.

That was on a Friday, and people prayed for me over the weekend. I had asked fellow students at my university, other actors in the show, and friends and family to be praying for me. I believed that God would heal me. Then except for getting up to do the stretching, I was basically bedridden during the whole weekend. The stretches helped. I also used heat on my leg, which helped some to loosen it up.

The following Monday, I was on my feet quite a bit, so my injured leg was getting really sore. The weekend rest and stretching had helped, but with being back on it again on Monday, I saw some decline in recovery.

Later that day in rehearsal, somehow I twisted my leg just a little bit, sending things downhill again for me. I was in a lot of pain—so much pain that I found it hard to get back to my dormitory. I had to walk across the entire campus to get there. With stairs and ramps, I found it extremely difficult to walk that far in so much pain. I was starting to get a little impatient for God to heal my hamstring. I went to bed and quickly fell asleep. Usually it takes a while for me to go to sleep, but that night was different.

I started into a dream where I was performing in *Bright Star* at ORU, and yes, it included participating in all the dances that I do. In my dream, one person—just one—was in the audience. I don't think I realized who it was. This guy was clapping the entire time, hooting and hollering—not really good theater etiquette, but there he was.

So in my dream, I went through the whole show. I just had a blast dancing and doing everything I could for God. And it was amazing, with a standing ovation afterward from that one guy. When I awoke, I got up, put on some shorts, and suddenly realized my leg was completely healed!

In years past, I had received what I'd call little healings here and there, with perhaps a little bit of doubt still in my mind. But in that moment I became completely convinced of God's healing power, and the experience was amazing.

I felt no pain, whereas before I could barely walk, it hurt so bad. I had full mobility. I started freaking out in my room. I shook my roommate awake to say, "My leg is healed!" Then I jumped. I did jumping jacks and then a squat—all that crazy stuff.

This healing of my hamstring is the biggest, most significant healing I've ever received. It was so significant because the injury was really affecting my ability to perform, work out, and do what I needed to do day by day. After my dream and the healing, rehearsals for *Bright Star* went great—as if the injury had never happened. The shows themselves went off perfectly, and I don't have any problems to this day with my hamstring.

As to the dream, may I first say that I can usually remember just parts or vague details of my dreams. This one, however, was unique. My recall was very vivid and specific. I have never had this experience before or since. I felt it was God—my Father and Jesus both—who was wildly applauding me.

—Anonymous

BE ENCOURAGED: The phrase "God is watching" shouldn't evoke an image of someone trying to catch us doing wrong. God is for us, not against us. He cheers our efforts—wildly.

He Watches Over Me

Megan's Story

I do not remember much about the actual wreck, and I do not remember any pain.

I'm told that on impact with the other vehicle at Highway 59 and Old Uniontown Road, my brother and I busted through the car's rear window. Jared and I were both thrown about twenty-five feet, but I must have landed headfirst. My oldest brother, Adam, and my grandma— both in seat belts—were okay, but Adam lost consciousness for a while.

Mom and Dad were working at the family restaurant, C&C Catfish. When a customer mentioned that traffic had backed up on Highway 59 due to a terrible wreck, my mom immediately grabbed the phone book. My grandma had left to drive us and drop Adam at a friend's birthday party, and now Mom desperately needed to reach that family.

The phone rang. "Mrs. Cluck," the voice on the line said, "your mother and children have been in a very bad automobile accident." My mom's scream silenced the entire restaurant.

Rushed to Crawford Memorial Hospital, I was immediately subjected to CT scans on my head and then airlifted to Arkansas Children's Hospital in Little Rock. The helicopter staff advised my parents to have someone drive there to meet me. As my mom, my uncle, and a cousin left Van Buren, people had already gathered at the hospital to pray. Praise God. Jesus said, "For where two or three gather in My name, there am I with them" (Matthew 18:20 NIV). And He was.

As they pulled in at Children's Hospital, the helicopter was coming in to land—it was a miracle that Mom made it so quickly and safely. I was still conscious, and Mom asked me this question: "Were you afraid in the helicopter by yourself?"

"No, Mama," I replied, "the man with the dark curly hair was right here." I held my hands above my face to show her. Surprised, Mom looked around. No one even slightly matched that description. When Mom asked if anyone else rode along with me in the helicopter, the helicopter team told her no. So she knew that "the man with the dark curly hair" was my guardian angel, whom God had sent to watch over me.

To this day, I can picture him. I do not remember seeing his body, but I recall a face—a male with tan skin and curly, dark hair—looking down on me. The angels God dispatches to watch over us are invisible, but in some cases He may allow us to see them. He did this for me when I was just six years old. Psalm 91:11 reads, "For He will command His angels concerning you to guard you in all your ways" (NIV). My guardian angel was there with me in that helicopter.

The nurses and doctors gave immediate attention to my severe head injuries, first sewing up a gash between my eyes and then conducting more CT scans. (My brothers, meanwhile, were released the next morning; Grandma broke one finger.)

In the first of many operations, surgeons reconstructed some of my skull's broken bones. Those around my nose would heal on their own, but I required a craniotomy. This involved removing part of the bone from my skull, exposing my brain. They surgically inserted metal plates to reconstruct my forehead, which had been completely crushed. The surgeons also installed a stent to drain fluids and relieve the pressure and swelling.

After a few days, the physicians reevaluated my broken jaw. When it looked like my mouth would need to be completely wired shut, it scared my mom. There in the waiting room, a sweet woman Mom knew stopped by to pray with her. God took care of it. The doctors needed to only partially wire my jaw shut—another prayer answered. In a week, the swelling was down on my head, and the matted blood could be washed from my hair. Also, the impact had lacerated my liver, but by God's grace, it healed on its own. After thirteen days, I got to go home.

The physicians expected I would have problems—both mentally and physically. God, however, had something better in mind. He had a plan and purpose for my life here on earth. He wanted to use me to glorify Him and live for Him. I will forever be thankful to Him. A few physical scars remain, but I view them as a reminder of God's amazing grace.

—Megan Graham, Arkansas

BE ENCOURAGED: We may not see the invisible realm around us until we need to. God and His angels are always there, though.

A Legacy of Faithfulness

Anita's Story

Growing up, I didn't see much of my grandparents. Our family was spread out all over the world. I was born in Venezuela to parents of missionaries, and we moved to Ecuador when I was eleven. My husband (whose parents were also missionaries in Ecuador) and I were married in Ecuador and have lived here serving the Lord for the past fifty-one years. I am grateful for the opportunities God has given us to work in the areas of education, health care, preaching, teaching, and administration through the years—and for our six children, their spouses, and seventeen grandchildren He's blessed us with along the way. But I'm also grateful for the legacy I have been given through faithful members of my family through the generations.

In the late 1800s, God's hand of healing started a ripple of missionary work in my family. My great-grandfather, Reverend John Waggoner, faithfully preached from the Bible and cared for the members of his congregation while also working as a butcher to support his family. On one visit to the hospital, John fervently prayed for God to give him strength to deliver devastating news to a young woman from his church named Zella, who had been diagnosed with spinal meningitis and was not expected to recover.

Holding back tears, John courageously entered Zella's room. But before he could utter the words, Zella let him know the doctors had already talked with her. John held her hand, and Zella announced she was ready to see Jesus.

At that moment two elderly women entered the room and asked for permission to pray with Zella. One read from Mark 16:15–18: "Go into all the world and preach the gospel . . . they will place their hands on sick people, and they will get well" (NIV). The other woman told Zella she believed in Jesus' power to heal. John and the women prayed together for healing for Zella. After the women left, Zella asked John if he believed God would heal her. He answered, "I'm a preacher of the gospel, but this is all new to me, Zella. But I learned long ago that I shouldn't limit God." In response, Zella told John that if God healed her, she would do anything He asked of her—*anything*.

After three days, John returned to visit Zella, only to find her hospital bed empty. She was walking and telling the hospital staff that God had healed her! She told John she was going to India to work with people with leprosy. And that's exactly what she did.

Several years later, Zella returned home for a visit and stopped by the Waggoner farm in western Pennsylvania, where John and his wife, Lulu, lived and raised a family.

They had fourteen children, one of whom was my grandfather, Harry Waggoner.

At the time of Zella's visit, Harry was just nine years old. While the adults visited, Harry sat in a cherry tree above them, listening. Harry was moved by Zella's words about the need for more missionaries to work with lepers in India. In that moment, Harry felt God telling him that someday he would serve God in India and bring help to the lepers.

When Harry finished eighth grade, he quit school and worked full-time on the farm to help his family. At age fourteen, he became deathly sick with pneumonia. His parents, fearing the worst (two of Harry's brothers had already died—one of German measles, the other of smallpox), prayed for the Lord to heal their son. In his bed, Harry silently prayed, telling God he would serve Him in India if God allowed him to recover. A few days later, Harry's temperature and breathing were back to normal.

In his late teens, Harry attended Bible school and received training in missionary work. He later married, and he and his wife, Helen, left for India. At this time in India, there were about 400 million people who did not know Jesus. Thousands—many of them lepers—were dying each day without hearing about the eternal healing that is found through faith in Jesus. Harry and Helen traveled from village to village, delivering tents and Bibles to people suffering from leprosy and teaching them from the Bible. During this time, they had nine children—including my mom, Almeta. They eventually raised enough money to buy land and used it to build a church, a clinic, and a residential building for lepers.

God's work of healing and the faithfulness of Zella and Harry have made a lasting mark on my family. I praise the Lord for His work in the hearts of people who answer His call on their lives.

—Anita Howard, Ecuador

*Some of the information from this story, including the quote by John Waggoner, is taken from *The Vow* by Hal Donaldson and Kenneth M. Dobson (Paramount, CA: Onward Books, Inc., 1991), 17–24.

BE ENCOURAGED: God has a purpose for you. He will safeguard your life until your work on this earth is finished.

My Constant Friend

I was what most people considered a good girl. I got good grades in school and didn't smoke, drink, or engage in wild partying. Yet just months before my thirtieth birthday, I found myself in a jail cell because of my own actions.

According to my mother, I was initially a happy, bubbly child who would embarrass her by introducing myself to strangers. But when I was about seven years old, that happy-go-lucky child permanently ceased to exist. I was sexually abused by a family acquaintance. I became a sad, often depressed little girl who did not see her own worth.

We moved from New York to Mississippi and stayed with my grandmother for a while. She took me to church, where I learned about God and became fascinated with the Bible. However, when we moved into our own place, I stopped going to church because my mom didn't go at that time. The lifeline I had found was taken away. I was still damaged, having had little therapy for the trauma I had experienced. I was a withdrawn child who found it hard to open up and trust people.

Fortunately, when I was twelve, my mom returned to God and we started going to church. I officially got saved and was baptized. I started carrying my Bible to school each day like a shield. Maybe I felt I needed the protection.

I was teased in school. I wasn't the prettiest little girl. I was shy and reserved. I didn't have the nicest clothes. And I was in Mississippi with my New York accent, a little black girl who "talked white" according to the kids. So even into my teen and young adult years, my low self-esteem stayed with me. And I searched for love in all the wrong places—looking for the dad who had never really been a part of my life, looking for someone to tell me I was good enough to be loved.

By this point in my early twenties, I had walked away from God. I married an ex-con who drank and was on drugs. He soon left me for another woman, but I hoped he would come to his senses and leave his girlfriend, whom I'll call Connie. However, he continued to see both of us.

One day I'd had enough and was determined to confront her about my husband. I invited her to my house, but I deliberately made her angry and we ended up fighting over a knife. I cut her pretty badly. I was arrested and taken to jail for aggravated battery.

While my parents were gathering the money to get me out on bail, the DA increased the charges to attempted murder. Not only that, but Connie had told him I wouldn't let her leave, so he charged me with kidnapping too. So I could no longer afford bail. I was stuck in jail until the trial.

I didn't realize at the time that the exaggerated charges were a blessing in disguise, allowing me to plead not guilty. But I was incredibly angry and wanted revenge. Rather than crying out to God, I became consumed with trying to figure out how to get out of there—and what I would do when I did.

After some time, I moved to a one-person cell, where a Bible sat on a bookshelf. Day after day, God kept calling to me to read it. Eventually, I listened. I found God again, and it was like meeting an old friend. I found Jesus and His life so fascinating and started taking notes. As I read the Bible, God softened my heart and convicted me that I needed to face the consequences for my actions.

So I forgot about my plans for revenge. I started going to church and Bible study at the jail, and later I started leading Bible study with some of the women.

During the trial, my husband, who had promised to testify on my behalf, simply backed up everything Connie had said. At that point, I had no hope that the verdict would be anything other than guilty!

I remember being in the holding room while the jury was deliberating, just leaning on God and making peace with whatever the verdict would be.

But the jury found me not guilty *on all counts*. I had been arrested because of my own actions, but God Himself declared me innocent and called me to a ministry of teaching the Bible. And He showed me that my notes on Jesus' life were actually the beginning of a book.

I often still feel unworthy of the things God has called me to do. But then I pick up my Bible and I am reminded that God has always been my constant Friend, that Jesus has always been my help.

I now hold a master's degree in biblical studies with plans to pursue a doctorate in biblical studies. God has allowed me to write and teach, and I'm also the cofounder of Route 66 Ministries, which is dedicated to helping people read and understand the Bible.

—Cynthia Austin Tucker, Florida

This story is adapted with permission from her forthcoming book, *Christians Get Discouraged Too.*

BE ENCOURAGED: Proverbs 24:16 says a righteous person falls but gets back up again. We're not defined by our failures but by our resilience. By the grace of God, we can continue to stand!

God Is Real

Kevin's Story

At my desk at the State Department in Washington, DC, I was told by coworkers of televised coverage showing that one of New York City's Twin Towers had been struck by a plane. An aviator with the US Navy, I concluded that an inexperienced pilot in a small craft had goofed up instrument flight conditions. But this theory didn't square with TV news showing a blue sky; there was no need for instrument flight. The impact of a second aircraft left no doubt. The United States was under attack. I was stunned.

Not long afterward, we received word that yet another aircraft had struck the Pentagon, with smoke rising from I-395 in Virginia. Exiting the State Department's security zone, I realized that my office complex could be a likely target as well. As I hustled toward the Pentagon, I noticed that traffic had stopped and the morning was eerily quiet. Like me, many people were in shock.

Passing Lincoln Memorial and crossing Memorial Bridge, I saw thick, black smoke rising from the Pentagon. These moments felt surreal, like a Tom Clancy novel about an epic event unfolding. Yet it was all too real. Imagining the numbers dead, I wanted to help. When I arrived at the

Pentagon's river entrance, a medical worker handed me a face mask.

I followed others. Once inside, visibility was minimal due to thick, white smoke. The Pentagon's structure was intact, with a fire raging out of control on the other side of those concrete walls. In addition to the white curtain, black smoke billowed forcefully and noisily into the sky. Firefighters battling the conflagration were setting strategy while others rested in the courtyard.

I was assigned to a stretcher team that was directed to accompany the firefighters and spirit away the injured as we encountered them. As the fuel fire raged, hours passed and our hopes of rescuing more victims faded to a more likely scenario—that of recovering victims' remains. After nearly twelve hours, we were relieved by National Guard soldiers. During my time in the smoke and haze, I had time to consider the day's ramifications. I was struck by the evil of the events.

Not exactly sure what evil was, I nonetheless could point to this day with certainty as a prime example. Events of the past, such as the Holocaust, Stalin's mass starvation, and the Killing Fields of Cambodia's Khmer Rouge, hadn't made sense to me. The ethnic cleansing of Bosnia and the genocide in Rwanda left me bewildered. How could people justify the murder of thousands or millions? I also pondered on whether God is real. And, if so, how could He let this horror happen?

My pathetic (truly almost nonexistent) relationship with God did not come close to helping me explain that day's events. I had been raised Catholic, but 9/11 shook my feeble beliefs to the core. This began my first serious search for truth about God's existence. I also considered the beliefs and practices of various religions and denominations. When I sought the Lord with everything in me, He began to answer me. I found that God is real!

Evil—both personal and structured—is that which opposes God's will. Moral evil affects human beings and their relationships with each other. Examples of evil and injustice abound: tyranny, genocide, human slavery, corruption, oppression, exploitation, torture, false imprisonment, organized crime, hate, murder, and religious persecution.

I have felt the power of the Holy Spirit in myself, and I have seen Him manifested in others. I have experienced a healing miracle. Diagnosed with severe sleep apnea, I'd stop breathing until awakened by lack of oxygen. But as I was prayed for by the power in Jesus' name, I received immediate healing.

The trauma of 9/11 led me on a search for the truth, which ultimately resulted in God's healing of my sleep disorder. But it didn't stop there. Because of these experiences, my wife and I have taken part in healing ministries. We have witnessed God's hand of healing in numerous ways—deaf ears hearing again, blind eyes regaining sight, cancerous tumors shrinking and disappearing, and more! And beyond physical healings, countless deep emotional inner healings have occurred right in front of my eyes.

What have I learned? God is real. Above all, I have learned, "Seek first His kingdom and His righteousness, and all these things will be given to you as well" (Matthew 6:33 NIV).

—Kevin Hutcheson, Missouri

BE ENCOURAGED: The kingdom of God— the pearl of great price—stands in brilliant contrast when surrounded by dark evils that this world holds. Ask God for His perspective on problems, whether large or small.

Our Family's Whirlwind and God's Mirror

Carmen's Story

As a little girl, I dreamed of being a wife and a mommy. I spent playtime imagining what life would be like with a family of my own. Married at age thirty, I agreed with Jeremy, my husband, that we would wait to start our family.

The time came when we decided to try to conceive a child. Jeremy may have expected fun and adventure, not the veritable science experiment I gave him—charts, counting, ovulation windows, and checking temperatures. Days turned to months without a positive pregnancy test, and then months became years.

At that point, things that never before had bothered me could send me into a tailspin of tears—a new baby announcement or an invitation to a baby shower (many of which I did not attend). Other things—family and baby pictures on social media, even diaper commercials—were hard to endure.

Learning to trust God regardless of whether a dream dies is completely different than believing Him when things are going well. During this season of life, I changed the way I prayed as I began to more fully understand what it means to be desperate for divine intervention.

Earlier in our marriage, Jeremy and I had invited kids who needed a place to live to stay with us. Not officially foster parents, we had hosted some fifteen kids in our home at one time or another. We've been passionate about foster care, certain that God had called us to advocate for vulnerable children and families. My infertility just fueled this fire in our hearts.

As a female with no biological children, still in child-bearing years and dealing with infertility, I had reached a point where I wanted to pursue adoption. God had put in me the desire to be a mom, and He had seen our eight years of trying to conceive.

Eleven weeks after Jeremy and I started foster parent training, we were officially certified. Less than two months later, we received word that our first placement would be arriving in the evening.

Nervousness, excitement, and a little trepidation accompanied me as I hurried home from work. I wanted to be there when the investigation team arrived. With a knock at the door, we opened it. In walked an absolutely beautiful blue-eyed, blonde-haired little boy.

You might feel inclined to ask, "What happened next?" Well, God handed me a "mirror." A year into Little Man's placement with us, the agency reunited him with his birth parents. His younger brother was born, and within a few months, both boys were placed in our home after their parents' relapse. The placement lasted a year before they were returned to the parents.

A youngest brother was born, and all three boys stayed with their birth parents for six months until another relapse occurred. This time when they came to us for care, they did not leave. I won't delve into the highs and lows of our emotional roller coaster during all of this. Before their arrival, we had taken in another beautiful baby boy. So now we were a family of six, with four boys all under the age of three. A whirlwind! It has been that way since, and we wouldn't change it.

A whirlwind and also a mirror. Who knew what foster care would usher me into? I entered territories that exposed flaws and faults inside of me so disheartening that I wanted to abandon everything in desperate sadness.

Nowadays, people tell us, "These boys are so blessed to be with you." I agree that Jeremy and I have played a huge part in ensuring that the boys know love, family, and safety. But we know who most needed the gifts of this journey. I am indebted to my heavenly Father for the life lessons He taught me during this season of our lives.

Four years after starting our foster care journey, we adopted David and Steven. The following spring we adopted their youngest biological brother, Robert. A little over a year later, we adopted our fourth son, Tylen. We ended our foster care license but continue to advocate for vulnerable children and families. We have joined with other foster families to develop a nonprofit organization. Its focus is faith-based foster family recruitment, retention, training, and long-term support.

—Carmen Howard, Missouri

> **BE ENCOURAGED:** God works in the seasons of our lives to teach us more about Him and about ourselves. Embrace every season, every moment, and look for the blessings God pours out when you least expect them.

Restored by God's Love

Devin's Story

Mom hung up the phone, turned slowly, and spoke to us, but her words made no sense to me. "Kids . . . I don't know . . . how to tell you this . . ." Tears coursed down her face. "But . . . your dad . . . just shot . . . and killed himself." A fog of sadness, despair, and hopelessness overwhelmed me. Then came fear, confusion, anger, and eventually numbness. This was a nightmare. Gone? And he *chose* to be gone? He *chose* to leave me? To abandon me?

I'm eleven! I screamed inside my head. *And I need my dad.* Even today, I lack the words for the pain, agony, and confusion of that time nearly thirty years ago. Amid the blur, though, my mind holds thoughts of a very specific moment. My brother, my sister, and I were lying on my mother's bed. "Kids, I don't know why this happened or why your dad chose to end his life," I remember hearing Mom say. "I don't know how we will get through this, but I do know that God will use this pain and hurt someday to bring glory to Himself and help to others who are hurting."

Like a darkness hovering everywhere, unbearable hurt lasted days, then weeks, and then months. Classes started again at school. The lies began to become my truth. I felt so rejected and abandoned by my father. His decision led me to believe that I wasn't good enough for him to want to choose life. I reasoned that if he really loved me, he would have chosen to stay.

I found myself asking, *Why was my dad's love for me not enough to keep him alive? Why was I not enough?* Questions of *Am I loveable? Valuable? Acceptable?* haunted me for years.

These questions consumed me. They drove my every decision. I sought in others—and in things—the love and acceptance I was missing from my father. People pleasing and perfectionism became my way of living. Shame became woven into my identity. Even as a young pastor's wife with small children, I still struggled with questions of *Who am I?* and *Am I good enough?*

That tragic day decades ago—the day the devil tried to destroy me—shaped my life. But God had a different plan and purpose for me. He meant to redeem me, and He has done just that. While I'd like to tell you the exact moment of my healing, I can't pinpoint just one moment. Over several years, God has patiently and tenderly removed the hurt, like peeling away layers of an onion (and I experienced the tears as He peeled these layers).

In His timing and in His perfect way, He has taught me. He freed me from the shame I had carried. In my weakest, most vulnerable moments, He is my strength. He has replaced lies of doubt and insecurity with His truths: I am lovable, acceptable, and valuable because I am His child. I no longer look to people or things to define me. I know I am 100 percent accepted by Him. I've been shown what a relationship with the very best Father is like. I share my story with others, and the words that my mother spoke over me have unfolded in such beautiful ways.

My favorite Bible verse says, " 'For I know the plans I have for you,' declares the LORD, 'plans to prosper you and not to harm you, plans to give you hope and a future' " (Jeremiah 29:11 NIV). God used a suicide that the devil intended for my destruction to instead restore me. The loss of my earthly father opened a door for the Holy Spirit to reveal to me the never-ending love and safety of my heavenly Father. I also like the verse that states, "We know that in all things God works for the good of those who love Him, who have been called according to His purpose" (Romans 8:28 NIV).

My mother's words of that tragic day are fulfilled in my story. Every time I share what God has done in me and through me, someone is helped. While I long for the memories of my earthly father, my heavenly Father has filled me with so much joy, peace, and hope.

—Devin Thomsen, Iowa

BE ENCOURAGED: God sees the end from the beginning. He also honors the prayer of people who care for us.

The Power of Prayer

D'Lynn's Story

We hurried to the emergency room with our fifteen-year-old son, Hudson. We had been hanging around downstairs at our house when suddenly the right side of his face was drooping. On his right side, he was losing feeling and vision.

He could only walk with a great deal of help from us. I never felt panicked. I called our church's House of Hope and Healing, where intercessors pray twenty-four hours a day, seven days a week. During our drive to the hospital, as many as a thousand people may have been praying for us. We could feel the Lord so strongly with us.

At the ER, Hudson was put in a wheelchair. The staff went into "Code Stroke" mode—a code that alerts the hospital personnel and stroke team members to start diagnosis and treatment of potential stroke just as soon as the patient arrives. It also prioritizes that person for such procedures as lab tests and the CT scanner.

The ER team took Hudson into the triage area and ran MRIs (magnetic resonance imaging), all the bloodwork, and EKGs (electrocardiograms). Over the course of about two and a half hours, the medical team could not find a problem. After five hours, Hudson had regained all strength in his right arm and leg. His right eye vision came back too. He passed all the motor skill tests given him. Everything appeared normal.

So we were sent home, but we were told to go the following day to Children's Mercy Kansas City to follow up. Upon calling the hospital, however, we were told we needed a referral. Contacting the ER, I learned that Medical Plaza Imaging Associates in Kansas City was awaiting our arrival. Apparently, it is one of the best neuroscience centers in the country.

A doctor walked in and said, "I guess you've heard the diagnosis."

We hadn't heard any diagnosis!

He told us that Hudson had a weakness in the carotid artery behind his eye.

In hearing about his serious condition and the next steps to expect, Hudson was just as solid as a rock. He never wavered in his faith. We experienced peace the entire time. The hospital staff immediately got him into surgery for an angiogram. We were warned to prepare for the worst, and I was invited by the doctor to view the procedure.

"I have never seen anything like this," the doctor said later as we looked at the screen. "I'm the only doctor in this hospital who performs this level of angiogram. I perform two hundred a week, and I have never seen anything like this."

Hudson had lost major blood flow to the right side of his brain for around two and a half hours. The dye they'd injected showed where the blockage had occurred, which resulted in the blood finding another path to the left side of his brain. We were told that this was typical of the body's response—trying to find a path. But the timing was simply amazing. If Hudson's time without that blood flow, and the oxygen it carries, had been even two minutes longer, he would have suffered a major stroke or worse.

"It's like there was a hand clenched on the back of his head at the exact right time," the physician told us. "The blood started flowing again just when it was needed. This is an absolute miracle!"

The doctors were amazed that, with his strength and all his vision, Hudson showed no signs of an incident a day earlier. A number of stroke specialists began monitoring him, and he became part of a study. His situation and its results were rare.

For some time afterward, Hudson couldn't ride on roller coasters or play his trumpet. Nowadays, there's really nothing that he's prohibited from doing. We were told by his nurse, "You all are living proof of a supernatural . . .

something." When doctors or nurses asked us what we did, I answered them, "We prayed."

—D'Lynn Watts, Missouri

BE ENCOURAGED: Studying the human body is just one way of capturing the wonder of God, His work in creation, and His love for us. The wonder of our Creator gives us reason to praise Him. "For You created my inmost being; you knit me together in my mother's womb. I praise You because I am fearfully and wonderfully made; your works are wonderful, I know that full well" (Psalm 139:13–14 NIV).

Worship in the Battle

Diane's Story

Never would I have thought I would have cancer. A routine mammogram revealed a small, previously undetected mass, and I went in for a biopsy.

When I received the call about my biopsy results, I was alone. Unable to reach my husband, I called one of our pastors. Her wise words helped me to refocus and gave me strength over the next few months: "Diane, we are not going to panic. This has not taken the Lord by surprise. You will get through this. God is faithful." I took a deep breath and began to walk through the days ahead.

There were times of fear. One particular morning, I was sitting across the breakfast table from my husband. I could feel darkness hovering over me. The fear was so overwhelming. I told Steve, my husband, "I can't breathe. Start talking."

"Diane, this is not about you. It is about the glory of God," he began. "And it is not a matter of *if* God will receive glory; it's a matter of *when*." As he was speaking, the darkness began to retreat, taking all the fear with it. I could breathe again. The glory of God changes everything!

In surgery, the mass and fifteen lymph nodes were removed. I went home later the next day. During the days and weeks that followed, my family and church family stayed close and provided an abundance of prayers, meals, cards, flowers, calls, visits, and support for us. God knew just when I needed each one.

Then on Thanksgiving Day, I had to return to the hospital with an infection. If that wasn't enough to deal with, we had other circumstances crop up in our lives. At that time, Steve and our son were struggling in their business of flipping houses. This was during a tumultuous time for the housing market. They had to quickly sell two houses to avoid claiming bankruptcy. To add to the financial challenges, we went through an Internal Revenue Service audit. With my husband needing to focus on the financial mess, I almost felt alone in my battle with cancer.

Thankfully, results of biopsies showed that my lymph nodes and margins (edges of where cancer had been removed) were free of cancer; chemotherapy was not needed. However, over six weeks I received thirty-three radiation treatments, and I was told to expect side effects. I had been told that it would burn my skin, cause gastrointestinal issues, and make me physically exhausted.

Because of the faith of my family and friends and the prayers they offered, I went through the treatments and never missed one day of work. My wonderful coworkers covered for me for a few hours in the mornings when I went to treatment. My skin did get a little pink, but I experienced no GI issues and only had two short periods where I needed to rest. God is faithful!

During the course of my treatment, worshipping God was one way I knew how to fight. I remember how good it felt after surgery to lift *both* my arms again in worship. God alone is worthy of honor and thanksgiving. Reading the Psalms also brought me comfort. God's Word served as food to my inner being when the enemy screamed so loudly. The Lord is a high tower, and I run to Him.

Battles come into our lives since we have an enemy who wants to crush our faith. So we fight by standing, declaring God's Word, worshipping, praying, believing Him, and being thankful that He will show Himself faithful. We surround ourselves with like-minded leaders and people who fight with us.

I have become more convinced that God takes everything in my life and works it for good. Did I pray for a miracle? Yes, but the one given to me did not happen instantaneously. Instead, it came over time and was given through God and the prayers of the people He placed in my life. It is because I went through this hard time that I can now encourage people who receive the same diagnosis as me—I tell them that cancer doesn't get the final word; Jesus gets the final word.

—Diane Dailey, Missouri

> **BE ENCOURAGED:** God is faithful, and there is hope. He will never leave our side, and He will bring victory!

The Ten-Year Journey

Laura's Story

They place in my arms a tiny, screaming stranger, thrashing and afraid. So begins our ten-year journey together. Telling of it, I include the hard and scary places, for these episodes make the joyful times all the more beautiful. No highlight exists without shadow, no resurrection without death.

Leaving the orphanage is our Day 1, begun with loss for her. On the plane to America, I rest for the first time in days as my husband attempts to calm our little girl. Watching him, a kind, young Indian woman speaks up and says, "You're a hero."

"This doesn't feel heroic," he says quietly. It feels like brokenness. Across an ocean lies the hope of family and wholeness, but we feel like we're swimming.

In our home, she doesn't seem to attach to us. She screams wildly in fear at times. In her crib, however, she clutches a sock—something reminding her of the orphanage—and sleeps. This is Year One.

Our adopted daughter's new siblings adore her, and she begins loving them back. Strangers feel drawn to her, even picking her up without asking. To those unlearned about attachment disorder, it reads as friendliness and warmth. We begin to set more boundaries, creating a bubble that she might one day associate as her own.

For a long time, I measure her trust by one thing—can she close her eyes and rest with us present? Not yet. She never sleeps on my shoulder, my husband's chest, or on a long drive to vacation. This is Year Five.

Learning is hard. The new little one and I gain a step and lose two, so the next morning we begin again. At times, her responses hearken all the way back to a dusty road outside the orphanage—responses in a primal part of her when suddenly, the raging goes silent and her eyes go distant. For minutes she is gone to a place I cannot get to. This is Year Seven.

I walk into her room to wake her. She doesn't move. Stepping closer, I fear what I might find. All I see are resting eyelashes, soft breaths on her puckered lips, and against her cheek, a clutched blankie. I cry because she's asleep. This is Year Eight. The day that she rests her head on my shoulder and drifts into peaceful dreaming, I do not want to put her down.

Our adopted daughter and I are different now than on Day 1. We don't battle for the same things that we used to. In some areas, gripping tightly is best; in others, open hands are better. Together we have figured these out . . . and we are still learning. She has always laughed, but her laugh is fuller now, less encumbered. Maybe mine is too. Perhaps this journey to rest requires letting go; things may need to die to find life.

There's a science to it. God's world has a little secret inside: Life requires death. We find it in the cycles of the Amazon rain forest. The most fertile region on the planet is fertilized by sandstorms in Africa. Billions of particles are carried from the Sahara across an ocean on the wind. Within a dust particle is a dead microorganism absolutely vital to the life of the rain forest, for within these microorganisms is phosphorus, an essential nutrient for plants. The Amazon cannot produce enough of this to sustain itself.

Millions of particles of our small deaths are now sprinkled over the new world we're trying to create together—a million places of surrender, letting go and openings of the hand. And life blooms. This is the secret of the journey. This is Year Ten.

We were never swimming in that ocean between loss and hope. We were carried, like the sands over the sea. Within our heavenly Father's plan and purpose in that storm, I was a little girl not trusting her Father and not giving in. I wanted the broken way, not a new way. But God made a way—His Son's death for an eternal spring of life. He continues to carry us toward fullness of life.

Death travels hand in hand with life, and our newest daughter has made me less afraid of the shadows and of places that need a little dying. I reach out to her; she reaches back. We keep walking.

—Laura Betters, Delaware

> **BE ENCOURAGED:** At times we must let go of what we grasp tightly . . . to take the hand of our Father.

Right Where God Wants Us to Be

Al & Jan's Story

When my father-in-law died, he had left my wife, Jan, a portion of the family's long-struggling business. An accounting firm that handled his estate indicated that the likelihood of a turnaround was slim and maybe it was time to close the doors.

With strong corporate backgrounds, Jan and I learned in our own assessment that product quality was high, with sufficient demand. We found Jan's family members reluctant to invest to add equipment and labor, even though we had told them such changes could help us see profits.

Jan and I put in these initial investments. We planned to use the property to obtain loans once things improved. We began working in the operation, and within a year, things were looking positive. When the business reached a strategic time to increase production, Jan's family members declined on signing off on a loan. As a couple, we had already burned through our personal savings. What to do? Let the business close or continue on?

We chose the business. Slashing our personal spending, we put every available penny into it. Profitability seemed to be staring us in the face, and yet we just couldn't seem to attain it. Soon enough, we fell behind on taxes and bills, both business and personal.

Family relationships became strained. We felt that we should hold the course that Jan and I had set. Was this arrogance or was it faith? I could hardly call it the latter, as I had long ago abandoned God. Achieving financial success, I had grown accustomed to decision making that did not include Him. In this newest venture, my pride had led me.

Jan, on the other hand, had long believed that God was at work amid the mess. She had started attending church and was doing daily Bible study. While she listened to God, I tried to fix it all myself, working seven days a week. She and I alone continued in the business as the only family members.

About this time, Jan said, "Even if you could work twenty-four hours a day without sleep, you couldn't fix this by yourself." She was right. Not long afterward, I dropped to my knees in the middle of the factory floor and surrendered the burden. Relinquishing control, I gave it to God. Curbing the long hours, I began attending church with Jan and reinitiated morning Bible study. Dusting off my long-shelved prayer life, I felt confident a change was ahead.

Indeed, a change did come; our situation took a turn for the worse. A legal battle over control of the business consumed the next four years. State and federal tax agents spoke with us, as we had not met our obligations. The utility company shut off our gas, and I was sued for arrears of credit card debt. From a human viewpoint our situation was hopeless, but in God's eyes, we were right where He needed us to be.

Our time with God showed us more clearly each day that our identity was not in the success or failure of a business. Our true identity is in Christ. With my pride pulverized, we were able to share our story when the business received visitors.

Jan and I would say that we were in the midst of a miracle. Whereas once the business had meant long working hours for me, it became somewhat of a refuge. When we told people our story, our listeners were willing to share theirs. We believe the transparency of our situation has given others the strength not to give up on whatever hardship they were facing.

Eight years have passed since we began with the business, and we are still struggling financially. Yet, we're mostly at peace on this journey. Human ability could not have sustained us over these past years. God provides daily what we need; He has since the beginning.

With the lawsuit settled, Jan now owns the business and property. She and her mother had become estranged during the turmoil, but that relationship has been restored.

God also restored our relationship with another estranged family member, who now has become instrumental in moving the business forward.

We continue to pray that in His time, God will heal the remaining relationships that were hurt during the last several years. He's continually healing us.

—Al & Jan Zucker, Ohio

BE ENCOURAGED: Hardship can break our destructive pride and turn us to God. Daily Bible time is as important as regular meals. God's Word helps us face life's circumstances.

Freedom from Fear

Felicia's Story

When I was pregnant with my first baby, Quinn, I struggled to cope in a stressful environment at work. The workplace planted in me the seeds of anxiety, which then found a fertile environment during pregnancy. Fearing the unknown—and not wanting to face scary issues and increase my anxiety—I did not go to one birthing class or research anything on birthing or even ask questions of my physicians. My passivity removed my ability to advocate—or to even think—for myself.

When Quinn was born, she was very colicky. She did not sleep or eat very well. My husband, Daniel, and I were unaware of the medical problems she was having, and we were equally unaware of my own mental health challenges. All of this created a perfect storm of intense anxiety.

For the first six months of our child's life, I did not take her out for a walk. I was afraid that a neighbor might be a sniper and might angrily shoot us. Unrealistic images and scenarios played out in my head. The anxiety was gripping. My doctor told me, "You're a new mom. Anytime you have a question, call me." Well, I had a new question every day; I called her *every single day* for two months.

Our daughter's colic placed me in a precarious position; my capability as a mother came into question by physicians I was talking to—to the point where I feared I would lose my daughter. Surface anxiety then grew into a deep-seated fear that gripped me spiritually, emotionally, and physically. I took a nosedive into the deepest, darkest places I've ever been to mentally. Fearful thoughts took their toll on my body. I experienced heart palpitations, and at times I felt like I was drowning and could not breathe.

People's advice—such as "Worry about nothing; pray about everything"—irritated me. I wanted to reply, "Listen! I'm dealing with intense anxiety." I also rejected physicians' advice about taking an antidepressant, since that would have meant that I wouldn't be able to breastfeed Quinn.

My husband and I found help through a community of people whose emphasis is natural and holistic. We began addressing environmental matters, such as what foods we eat, what we had in our house, and our living space. We were also setting boundaries in our lives—little boundaries, like "Okay, I'm not going to eat at Taco Bell six times this week. I'm going to eat an apple instead." We determined that we'd eat a home-cooked meal every evening. Making intentional, smart decisions about our lifestyle helped us pay better attention to our health and our parenting. It helped us focus on the things in life we could control.

Meanwhile, at an Arise conference at our church, a friend prayed with me for freedom from anxiety. I awoke the following morning with a serious anxiety attack. I asked God, "Why?" It came to me that I lacked wisdom and empowerment. So I began reading whatever I could on anxiety and seeking out people whose opinions differed from my own. I wanted to hear their stories, their thoughts, and how they came to their conclusions. I wanted their truth from their experiences.

Even though it wasn't easy, I know God walked me through my anxiety. He gave me a community of people who relate to my circumstances. He opened my eyes to environmental factors. Finally He gave me the courage to seek wisdom, to stop sweeping it under the rug.

As I'm writing this, I'm seven months pregnant with our second child and in a very different situation than during my first pregnancy. At twenty-four weeks, Daniel and I were stopping contractions—and I wasn't fearful. I told the doctor what was occurring, and its causes and my conclusions were confirmed. So we put preventive steps in place. And I'm not terrified.

—Felicia Goodman, Missouri

BE ENCOURAGED: The Bible puts it simply in three words: "Do not fear." How our obedience to this plays out in everyday life may differ from one individual to the next. There isn't just one single way that we find courage in the face of our fears. We must learn what works for us.

Healed by the One Who Sees Us

Naomi's Story

About the time I began college, I joined the camera team at my church and started filming once a week for three consecutive hours. When I began to get headaches, it was a first for me. Growing up on my parents' farm, I had not experienced problems with my eyes. I was an avid reader—still am—and had no trouble with seeing short or long distances. To play high school basketball, I had a physical examination, and my eyes tested 20/25.

I asked myself what was causing the headaches. Could it be the camera's viewfinder? Was it the focus assist feature (which turns edges of a focused object green)?

Did the problem correlate to panning the camera, following the pastor as he paced back and forth? I lowered the light of the viewfinder and the focus assist. At every possible opportunity to turn my eyes from the camera, I did. Nothing worked.

After about three months, I went in for an eye examination and the ophthalmologist diagnosed me with esotropia. This condition causes the eyes to attempt to cross; the muscles that control the eyes must work hard to avoid crossing. The glasses that he prescribed for me seemed to help for a few weeks, but when the headaches came back, they were worse than before.

While running the camera during church services, I would wear my glasses with sunglasses over them. I still suffered awful headaches that would wipe me out for the rest of the day. I found lighting changes—entering the sunlight from a dim building, for example—excruciating, even when wearing sunglasses. Light fixtures blurred and streaked when I looked at them. My eyes often felt as though the liquid around them were thick and syrupy.

A memorable episode occurred on the first and only time I attended a concert. Seated in the balcony, I was directly in the path of a big, roving spotlight. Most of the time it was flashing in my eyes, but at times the light beam remained fixed—shining right at me. Needless to say, I did not enjoy the concert experience.

As the headaches continued for six months, I tried to avoid bright things, hardly ever looking higher than eye level. Any glimpse of direct light was pure torture. I kept getting dizzy, and on one Sunday at church I nearly fell off the camera platform. After that near miss I decided to leave the camera team.

By this time, I had decided to accommodate the headaches and other symptoms the best I could and move on with life. Then one evening our young adult group met for cocoa and fellowship. A couple from the church spoke, followed by people in our group talking about their recent experiences with God.

Somehow we next turned to praying for specific healings. Through all of this, the lights were stabbing into my eyeballs. I asked for prayer, and the thirty or so young adults gathered around me. One girl prayed for me as the others silently prayed to God in agreement.

I was overwhelmed. My body lost all tension, and I crumpled and fell down. My sister caught me so that I wouldn't land on the concrete floor. I had closed my eyes. Waiting a moment to open them, I told myself firmly, "I will be healed." When I looked up toward the lights, there was absolutely no pain, no blurring, nothing. My eyes worked as well as they ever have.

Relieved that the pain was gone, I started crying. I cried so hard, in fact, that my sister needed to explain to the others. She said that my eyes had been a source of pain lately, and that for months, I had been avoiding lights. I was one of several people healed by God that night.

Several months later, I needed to have my eyes treated for conjunctivitis, otherwise known as pink eye. My examination included testing my sight, with results showing 20/20—better than my high school sports physical. God had not only healed me, but He made me better than I was before. I thank God for the healing when I look around and experience no pain. I haven't needed glasses since I was healed.

—Naomi Scoggin, Missouri

BE ENCOURAGED: "For the eyes of the Lord range throughout the earth to strengthen those whose hearts are fully committed to Him" (II Chronicles 16:9 NIV). God sees us in our struggles, and He longs to heal us and bless us.

God Sends Us His Peace

Mackenzie's Story

The moment the wand of the ultrasound was placed on my pregnant belly and the picture appeared on the screen, I knew it. The progress of our twelve-week-old baby wasn't what it should be. Flooded with emotion, I looked at my husband. Our young daughter was also in the room. At age four, she had been praying since age two for a baby sister.

"Mama, did we lose the baby?" my daughter asked. I nodded my head yes, and all of us cried together. We named our baby Jordyn Shalom Love, which means "descending down in peace."

She stopped growing at about seven weeks—just after my first appointment with the midwife. My uterus was measuring fifteen weeks, since my body had not responded to the baby's death inside. It was called a "missed-miscarriage." I was scheduled for dilation and curettage (D&C) to remove the baby from my womb.

Phone calls followed, along with a public social media post to update everyone on our devastating news. We had told others immediately when we knew we had conceived, but now that we had lost this baby, I realized why people choose to wait to announce a pregnancy.

As I was anaesthetized before the D&C, a wave of peace and joy came over me. It could only have come from God Himself. Afterward, I told my husband, mother-in-law, and friend, and we all cried together, feeling God's goodness.

Two weeks later at a follow-up appointment, I learned that the miscarriage was due to a partial molar pregnancy. Jordyn wouldn't have been able to survive. The problem was because of additional hormones that my body had produced during the pregnancy. Rapidly multiplying cells can cause tumors in the placenta. The pregnancy had put me at high risk of cancer. I began undergoing weekly blood draws to check my human chorionic gonadotropin (hCG) levels to determine whether cancerous cell growth had occurred.

If chemotherapy were needed, we faced the chance that it would wreak havoc on my reproductive system. I told a lady at church about possible chemo and an end to child-bearing. Looking me square in the eye, she said, "Well that is not going to happen." I was filled with faith and knew that she was absolutely right. As heartbroken as I felt about losing a baby and equally heartbroken about the thought of never carrying another baby inside me, I knew I needed to lean on God and place my complete trust in Him.

By the fifth week of testing, my hCG level was negative. A number of physicians at the OB-GYN office had reviewed this quick drop in my hormone levels. The numbers showed that chances of cancer growth were almost nonexistent. Through my phone I heard these words: "I believe you are clear to try for another baby with your next cycle."

Within two months, I became pregnant. An ultrasound at six weeks showed a normal, healthy baby. At our second prenatal appointment, however, no heartbeat could be heard and no ultrasound technician was working. We spent the weekend feeling anxious and upset, yet trusting in God to protect our baby. The following Monday, as soon as the technician placed the wand on my belly, we saw a fully formed baby kicking, stretching, and moving around. We praised God and were so thankful to be past that scare. After nine days, we got a call to say that my blood test results were normal and that we were expecting a baby girl.

I gave birth to our sweet daughter Annabelle. She was healthy and happy. Overjoyed, I held her in my arms as I heard our son yell to his sister, "I think Mom just had the baby!" What an amazing and redemptive moment.

Even amid the hurt of losing baby Jordyn and the fear of the possibility of a cancer diagnosis, God's peace was upon me and I knew that somehow our story wasn't over. God would work this out for good. Our family walked into a new season of victory together. Because we went through this, we are a stronger, more united family and we're able to better share God's love and compassion with those who are going through difficult times.

—Mackenzie Love, Missouri

BE ENCOURAGED: Nothing can limit God. He is much higher and more powerful than anything in our lives. He can be trusted. He is good.

God Never Leaves Us

Brenda's Story

As a child, I felt so fortunate to have my parents together. Many of my classmates had such different situations. However, things began to shift at home during my junior high years, and I knew that my parents were struggling. Each would come to me to air their grievances about the other.

The entire foundation of my life was crumbling and falling apart, and I didn't know how to handle it. I started failing classes at school and acting out emotionally. I was no longer a carefree kid. I felt out of control. The oldest of three children, my childhood quickly faded. Placed on an antidepressant medication, my emotions began to level out. More hard times were ahead. My parents' divorce was finalized during my high school years.

Having wrestled with life's circumstances for several years, I was left weary, bitter, and harboring an unforgiving spirit. I had grown up attending worship services and youth events every week, along with going to summer church camps. However, it wasn't until a high school classmate invited me to her youth group that I began to seek God. With support from new friends and a church community, I started to experience Him for myself. He became real to me. No longer only the God of my parents, He became my heavenly Father, my safe refuge. He began to heal my wounded heart and rebuild a stronger foundation for my life.

My situation did not change overnight. Daily I chose forgiveness over bitterness. The Lord lifted off the heaviness and depression that I was carrying. He filled me with joy and life. Eventually—I'm not even sure when—I was able to go off the medication.

Continuing into adulthood, I moved to a new city. Feeling knocked around by life, I found myself isolated and depressed. At my new church, I was seeking God and getting small breakthroughs but couldn't seem to sustain the freedom for very long. My job site carried a negative atmosphere that led me further and further into a downward spiral.

I became numb. I shut down, even reaching a point at which my face wore no real expression. My eyes were empty, lacking any spark of hope or life. With hopelessness suffocating me inside, I couldn't breathe or break out of the stupor. Though I wanted to be happy and softhearted again, I lacked strength to get free.

I was again prescribed an antidepressant. I felt as though I needed medication to begin making strides to overcome my difficulties. I started looking for another job. For my emotional health, I needed a better work environment with a supportive boss and coworkers. The Lord opened up an amazing opportunity. This new job was a safe harbor where I could take refuge and begin to heal. I wrote declarations to myself, putting them up at home and work. I spoke these statements out loud every day, reminding myself of who God is and who He says I am. I stood firm on His Word and promises.

While continuing on medication, I also received more prayer at church. Close friends helped me fight for my freedom and healing from depression, attacking negative generational ties that entangled me. I decided not to accept them in my life anymore. I sought prayer whenever it was offered at church and began experiencing deeper levels of freedom than ever before. Hope began to return.

I was able to smile again, and life began to radiate from me. I rediscovered a desire to serve others and began doing so with joy. Although it took many years of work and trusting God, my relationship with my parents has been restored.

I am no longer on medication, but my emotional life is both a journey and a discipline. I often have to stop and ask myself, "How much sleep am I getting? What kinds of things am I eating, and how does this affect my energy level? How many consecutive sappy love movies have I watched? How much time have I spent alone lately? Is it time to reach out to friends and make fun plans?" I still have to make sure I am taking care of myself so I can continue on a healthy path.

While I've spent many years of my life feeling hopeless, God never left me. I always felt Him there, encouraging me, growing me into the person I am today. And while I may not ever know why my journey has involved so much emotional pain, I do know that if I continue to trust in God, He will create beauty out of ashes.

—Brenda Cline, Kansas

BE ENCOURAGED: Seek professional help if you need to. There is no shame in reaching out. That's why therapists and counselors are available. And trust God to help you stay on a healthy path.

A Journey of Surrender

Anonymous

Have you ever felt as though you could barely make it through a day? For a long time, this was my situation. Along with the responsibilities of my full-time job, I was dealing with the demands of being a wife, mother (of two toddlers), a friend, daughter, sister, and more.

Ready for a pursuit of joy, I didn't even know how to start the race. How could I pick myself up? In a very heavy fog for a long time, I sometimes wondered whether God intended to leave me in this situation forever.

What was the purpose of all this suffering? I remember deep feelings of loneliness, as well as assessing myself as not good or strong enough. Many people would describe the experience as a "dark night," when you know that God is there but you just can't feel Him.

A swirl of sickness seemed to engulf our family as never before. My mom had surgery; my husband contracted Lyme disease. I was first diagnosed with diabetes, then months later a second diagnosis. This time it was liver disease. Long silences from family, friends, and coworkers accompanied this period. People didn't seem to have the words of comfort and encouragement that I longed to hear.

Did I stop believing? Did I stop trusting? No, of course not. However, if I were asked whether my trust was completely in God alone, I would need to honestly answer, "Well . . . at times." During this time I kept hearing the word *surrender*. Over a period of five years, God had been taking me on a journey of total trust—a trial, really, in which I give up control; I surrender.

I wasn't sure what surrendering to God would mean for me—someone who was newly married and a new mom who had moved 1,400 miles away to a new country with a new language. I had a new job, a new family, no friends, and so many changes all at the same time. I can look back on that experience now and know that I was being prepared under His perfect plan and in His impeccable timing. This was a busy time of high stress and, in summary, it was overwhelming. However, it was also a very exciting time with new challenges and much learning. I could also identify within myself a very strong desire to please God and give Him control.

Several months ago, God revealed in a very sweet and gentle moment what He has been preparing me for. He showed me the most powerful gift imaginable. I experienced His healing. In the middle of my daily work, I could no longer ignore the neck pain from a car accident I'd experienced two months earlier. I had been getting treated for the injury, but it was not appearing to improve. I felt very helpless over this at times and, quite honestly, hopeless.

"Are you okay?" I was asked.

"Just a little pain," I answered.

"Can I pray for you?"

I said yes. In the back of my mind, I thought that one more prayer would be wonderful.

"May I touch your neck in the place where you are hurting?" was the next query.

"Sure." And I showed the injured area.

What followed was the shortest, most specific, and simplest prayer I have ever heard: "Lord, You know her pain. Please heal her. In Your name we pray, amen."

Our eyes were closed. As we opened them, I was asked, "How do you feel now?" My pain was instantly gone—none at all! In that very moment, I knew exactly what had just happened and I was brought to tears. I couldn't control myself.

Ever since the Lord healed me, that discomfort has not returned. I do not know if this healing is permanent. The pain could come back. However, I do know that God brought me to a point of surrender to Him. On my part, the healing was effortless; He did it all for me because that is how He loves us.

God has revealed His healing power in a very specific and strong way. As I still struggle in other areas of health, I believe He can do it again. I believe in the power of prayer. I believe that He continues acting through people as instruments of His love and that whatever we may face, He has surrendered Himself upon the cross to give us life, to heal us. I will keep on praising Him, for His mercies are new every day. To Him be all the glory, now and forever.

—Anonymous

BE ENCOURAGED: Surrendering to God makes us open and willing to receive all that He desires for our lives. It allows us to accept His love and His care in ways we never thought possible.

There Is a Way

Salmon's Story

It should have been a celebrative night during Chinese New Year, yet I wasn't home at 11:00 p.m. On a busy expressway, I staggered out of my car with a pounding headache. I could hardly recognize my car, which was now badly smashed by two other cars. I was told to seek medical attention without delay. At the hospital, the doctors conducted comprehensive tests on my neck and spine.

Nothing had prepared me for what I was told. Besides several torn tissues along my spine, the preliminary tests showed a lesion and a 2 mm cyst on my liver. A subsequent CT scan confirmed their presence. The physicians outlined several possibilities for the lesion: a benign growth, liver cancer, or signs of final stage cancer. The word *cancer* shocked me to my core. Sent home from the hospital, I could not bring myself to break the news to my wife and our four daughters. Sleepless, I prayed for peace. When I finally gathered the courage to tell my wife and children, we prayed together every day.

The possibility that I might leave my wife and young children behind prompted more sleepless nights. I'd watch my wife and daughters sleep, turning over in my mind every detail about them that I loved. Trying to come to terms with death, I set about to create a "daddy documentary" to show our girls how to fix things around our home—I wanted them to still see me when I was no longer around.

Before my surgery, I joined the local scouts on a hike. As we hiked, I observed a growing storm. Then torrential rain started falling not far from where we'd hiked. Oddly, the rainstorm never caught up to us. Like the pillar of cloud that guided the people of Israel in the Bible's Old Testament, this rain cloud moved when we moved but stopped when we stopped. This experience opened my eyes to God's assurance of His presence and power—even His power to heal me.

That night, my wife and I prayed for healing. "Give me another forty years," I told God, "and I'll live differently for You."

Soon after, I had the final MRI scan for surgery. When I met with the specialist to receive my scan result, he told me that the lesion had disappeared! Seeing my doubt, the specialist showed me that all that the scan picked up was the tiny cyst. The images were acceptably sharp enough to detect it. God had removed the threat of cancer.

I was then working as a senior officer in the Singapore Prison Service. This had been my job for eleven years. I started to ask God how I would live differently for Him. I prayed for guidance.

The following month I received a call from a friend, a prominent psychologist, Dr. Thomas Lee, whom I had not heard from in twenty years. We reconnected, and through his mentoring, I gained clarity of my desire to help people—especially the underserved populations and missionary families—through the difficulties of their lives.

Leaning on my faith in God, I quit my job and applied to be trained as a marriage and family therapist at Wheaton College in the United States. Despite poor odds, God opened doors that allowed my family to obtain visas (seeing as we are from Singapore) and allowed me to gain a tuition scholarship. With our limited resources, we wondered how we could sustain our living until I gained my licensure as a therapist. It is almost crazy to think that we would pull ourselves out of our comfort zone to live without certainty of the next step. It was a bold decision to leave our familiar home, but we trusted that when God leads, there is a way.

Indeed, God knew our needs. We received a car from new friends on our third day after arrival in Illinois. When our savings reached a critical low, we received an unexpected lump sum of money as a settlement for my neck injury in the accident. The amount was enough to cover our house rental for three years—not less than we needed, and not more.

We have faced difficult situations and challenges as foreigners, but God has never left us. Looking back, living by faith and obedience is an unregretful step for me and my family in experiencing the reality of God's power, grace, and faithfulness.

I have no doubt that God used the wreck and the medical scare to get my attention, to remind me who was ultimately in control. And now He has me leaning on Him for everything as I seek His will for my life.

—Salmon Chung, Singapore

BE ENCOURAGED: God is faithful to guide us as we take a next step of obedience to Him. There is a way—when you let God lead the way. The question is, Will you then move forward in confidence?

Our Amazing Father

Pat's Story

I grew up in a home that from the outside looked normal. That wasn't the case. My father sexually assaulted me from the age of three to around thirteen and once again when I was eighteen. My mom emotionally abused me by repeatedly saying I ruined her life. I got to the point where I hated myself. I hated God. I hated everything.

I started cutting to take away the emotional pain, but it didn't help. I went to a Bible college to run away. But the pain was still there, and I tried to commit suicide. My parents made me come home. Desperate for an escape, I married someone who I believed really cared about me and was my way out. But it wasn't true love. After four rocky years, it ended.

I fell into depression and again tried to commit suicide. I called my ex-husband to take the kids for a short time. He tried to get full custody at that point because I was not in good enough shape mentally or physically to take care of our kids.

I ended up living on the streets and crashing at friends' houses. Over the next several years I tried to commit suicide over a dozen times. Things were bad enough that I ended up in the hospital. I couldn't understand why it wouldn't end.

During this time, a friend talked me into speaking with a pastor who was also a counselor at a local church. I was angry before I ever walked into her office, angry during our meeting, and angry as I left. I swore I would never go back. Shortly after, I attempted suicide again and was in hospital lockdown. To my surprise, that same pastor showed up. I got to thinking she must not be too bad. We started talking, and I slowly began to trust her. She convinced me to visit the church a few times. I was still angry. Still very angry at God over how my life had gone.

I was searching for that acceptance, but I didn't know how to reach out. The pastor eventually set me up with a couple from church who regularly picked me up. I would go to church with them and sit quietly by myself. They kept showing kindness to me—something that was so new to me. But the wall was still up. I would sit quietly, not reaching out. If someone said hi, I would say hi back, but that was all.

I started meeting with the pastor more regularly, and she recommended I go through a small group discipleship program. I had heard of it before. She said it would be difficult and that I would have to go back to the beginning and relive and work through everything from my past. Well, I did. I was dealing with the anger. I was mad at God. Mad at my dad. Mad at my mom.

When we got to the close of the first phase of the program, I started to recognize a change in myself. I learned that God loved me. People loved me. Through my church and my small group, I found out that I was truly loved by others. It was amazing!

I started participating more in small group and at church. I started praying and letting God into my life. Through that discipleship program God has helped me open up so much so that He could bring down the walls I had built around myself. God is an amazing Father. And I thank Him every day because without Him I would not be healed. I truly believe I'm being healed by God still today. He's changed my perspective on life. My love and understanding of God are so much clearer now.

Life is wonderful. Yes, there are struggles, but God is right there with us in those struggles. He has changed my way of thinking toward others. I relate with people in a totally different way than I used to. I recognize that I need to reach out to people if I want people to reach out to me. By reaching out to people, I hope to show them how Jesus has changed my life. He has made me a better person and a better friend. I have let the walls down so much because of what Christ has done. All people are not out to hurt me.

It has not been an easy path. Accepting the truths of the Bible and what it looks like to live life in Christ and by the power of His Spirit is hard. I wanted to give up many times. But, I'm so glad I didn't because if I had, I would not be where I am today, healed from my past and resting in the perfect love and peace of Jesus.

—Pat Evans, Iowa

BE ENCOURAGED: God uses loving people in our lives to help us heal. Don't be afraid to trust someone who genuinely cares, and be ready to allow others to trust you. Most of all, trust in God, your amazing Father who offers you His healing and peace.

Healed in the Name of Jesus

Shaunda's Story

Oh, I suffer. In fact, I have been hospitalized frequently due to my condition. But please don't see my condition. Instead, see me—a fighter, healed, surviving and standing in the power of Jesus Christ.

Just after my birth I was admitted to the Arkansas Children's Hospital, where specialists diagnosed me with congenital adrenal hyperplasia (also called CAH or adrenal insufficiency). With my adrenal glands clinically dead, I was prescribed steroids. My endocrinologist was Dr. Joycelyn Elders, who later served as United States Surgeon General. She told my parents of my case's severity and estimated that I'd live to age eleven, possibly with mental and physical disabilities.

I remember Momma and Daddy taking me to be prayed for. I knew the Lord and believed in prayer. Ours was a large family, and I loved them. One brother had died at just ten days. His body needed salt. Similarly, mine is a salt-wasting condition. My parents treated me differently than they did my seven siblings, fearing my early demise.

However, after passing my "death sentence" age, I began thinking about my future. I finished school, got a job, and got married. Several years ago, my husband and I were five months away from adopting our daughter, Emileigh, when I was admitted to a hospital with kidney sepsis. The following month I was hospitalized with pneumonia.

Months before these hospitalizations, God had been speaking to me about being a stay-at-home mom. I rejected this, being heavily involved in my work. I found my identity in my career. Why leave that when daycare is an option for the child we were going to adopt? In my hospital room, though, I gave in to God, telling Him I would not test Him but instead trust Him. I left the hospital room that day and became a stay-at-home mom.

While going in and out of hospitals, I began talking with the staff about the love of Christ. When people would say, "You are glowing," I'd reply, "Let me tell you why." I had opportunities to pray with countless nurses, patients, and their families. Tears would stream down their faces as I spoke with God about their situations. These are the people I continue to pray for today—nurses, housekeeping workers, dietary therapy staff, and more.

Later, after a routine pain management injection, I had trouble. By the next month every nerve in my body was lit up in excruciating pain. It began to affect my adrenal condition. An emergency room staff drew blood samples, and results showed a low sodium level.

Comparing blood results with those of my endocrinologist two months earlier, I pointed out differences to the ER physician. "Well, I don't see anything wrong," the doctor said. I extended my hand to shake his and said, "You have just viewed the blood results of a forty-two-year-old steroid-dependent CAH patient with low sodium. Do you think my red blood cells being through the roof is why I have nerve sparking?" He immediately started an IV into my vein, which had collapsed, and scheduled hospitalization. He let me delay being admitted until after a school event with one of our two adopted daughters.

Returning to the hospital, my condition had worsened. I was septic, my blood infected. A phlebotomist named Vangie came at 1:30 a.m. to draw blood. We had already become close during earlier sessions. I had prayed for her and she for me. Now, even as my pastors, Bettye and Billy Nickell, prayed on the phone with me, Vangie was doing the same in my room. We called out to God Almighty for my healing.

Addressing the infection directly, Sister Nickell said, "In the name of Jesus I command this infection and pain to go back down and exit the same way it came in." The terrible feeling went down my spine and left my body. I was healed by God's power. Blood test results showed no infection. I left the next afternoon and have not experienced that fiery pain since. I thank God for His healing throughout my forty-two years of life and into eternity.

From being told that I wouldn't live past age eleven, to having a career, a husband, and beautiful kids and then surviving a blood infection, I think it's pretty obvious that God controls my destiny. The diagnoses delivered do not define me. And while I still monitor and adjust my potassium, sodium, and magnesium each day, God is walking me through this every step of the way. And I am eternally grateful.

—Shaunda Adams, Kansas

> **BE ENCOURAGED:** God sees our suffering and understands it well, for Jesus, His Son, was the Suffering Servant foretold in several chapters of the Old Testament book of Isaiah. He suffered on the cross for our sins. The hands that were nailed to the cross are the hands that save and heal today.

A New Man

Dad wasn't a believer. In our little family, faith in God first came to me, then to my sister, and then to Mom.

Throughout my youth, we were besieged by different sicknesses. I had a blood disorder at the age of seven or eight. My red blood cells collapsed, and if I hadn't been taken to the hospital on time, I could have died. My treatment consisted of IVs and transfusions.

Dad came to a point of saying, "God, if You'll save my son, I'll serve You." That commitment was made long ago. God did it; He healed me and I survived that health crisis, only needing periodic injections afterward. But Dad did not follow through on his pact with the Lord. Without really understanding the Bible, he didn't know where to turn. He didn't get it like he needed to.

Growing up hunting and fishing, I could look around and say, "Okay, this is too vast and too perfect for there not to be a God." There needed to be more than the physical world. But I had no idea that God wanted to have a relationship with me. Besides, I was sort of wandering through life, finding my identity in sports and other pursuits. In my high school years, our family was doing all right when suddenly everything started to fall apart. Dad's work decades earlier as a lifeguard was catching up to him, as he saw a physician regularly to have cancers cut off his skin. He needed this over a period of years.

Dad carried inside a tension that would flare at times, affecting Mom. She became depressed and suffered anxiety due to my dad's selfishness. He loved us, but there was always an underlying anger and that snap. Both of my parents were teachers. Dad taught at a small school that was being consolidated with another, so he lost his job. He had a master's degree, which made finding work more difficult as schools could instead hire those fresh out of college. My parents were going to lose the house without his income. Financial difficulties accompanied the illnesses that our family endured.

"You know what, God? We're sick," Dad finally said. "My family is ill. Hunter has a hole in the base of his spine; his sister, Tia, has an incurable disease. If You're real, be real to me now." He began to seek the Lord five or six hours a day. At that point, God turned everything around for our family. As Dad began to read the Bible, God poured into him an understanding of the words. My dad started to talk to others about the Lord. I was about seventeen years old when I witnessed a transformation take place in him.

The hole near the bottom of my back for a couple of years was a cyst about three-fourths of an inch deep. This needed to be packed with medical gauze. Taking his Bible one day, Dad showed me a dozen verses from Scripture that addressed healing. When he prayed for me, nothing happened right away, but he pronounced healing over me. When I awoke the next day, that hole was completely sealed shut.

I was struck by the Lord's power, and it changed everything. Experiencing that love—when you haven't done anything for Him or served Him and you don't deserve this love—transforms a person. You become a totally different person.

Some level of disappointment and discouragement in my faith came to me afterward when I ran into people with different views about God's willingness to heal people. As Dad began to talk with people about God's goodness, he was met with doubt, unbelief, fear, and hurt. It was interesting to face that kind of negativity after having seen the Lord's work in me. I'm reminded that I need to go directly to the Word of God to receive the truth about God and His power to heal.

—Hunter Driscoll, Missouri

BE ENCOURAGED: The Bible tells us that "if anyone is in Christ, the new creation has come: The old has gone, the new is here!" (II Corinthians 5:17 NIV). It is a privilege to see this happen in others. When it happens within us, it is exhilarating.

Jesus in the Hole

Cristi's Story

I guess I always knew there was a problem down deep. Even as a child I remember secretly wishing I had a broken leg. I don't have the traumatic tales that others do. I was never abused. We were not poor. We always had food on the table. And a white picket fence. But that doesn't mean I lived happily ever after.

On my fifth birthday my mom and dad drove me to my aunt and uncle's home to celebrate my birthday. I received a ballerina cake and a white dress. And then it happened— my parents packed up my siblings in the station wagon and drove away while my uncle held me tightly. I kicked and screamed and cried. My parents never looked at me while they pulled out of the driveway. I still remember my little sister staring at me, probably wondering if our parents would leave her too.

My little heart broke that day. And though I lived a very good life filled with school, friends, and days at the lake, I had suffered irreparable damage. I somehow reasoned at five years of age that I must have been abandoned because I wasn't perfect enough for my family. I would never make another mistake. I would be perfect the rest of my life—straight A student, responsible in every way, hard worker always. This was my identity, but underneath was a shattered heart. And shattered hearts find a way to be heard.

It all went seemingly well for a while—on the outside. I married, had a family, and worked a successful job. Somewhere in there I had a miscarriage, and I cried for six months. But that seemed normal to everyone around me. Then I had an affair and tried to commit suicide. I told the nurse and doctor it was all a mistake. Somehow, they believed me. I tried to contain the madness. It would work for a couple of years, then resurface again in another way.

My vulnerable soul had sustained irreparable damage. And though I tried every angle I knew—prayer, laying on of hands, retreats, praise, faith, words—the pain inside only grew. I didn't want to admit that nothing was working to heal my broken heart. I had nowhere to turn—until someone listened to me. *Really* listened. Sat. Felt. Stayed. It was respite that allowed me to breathe. And so I took a deep breath.

Little did I know that breath would lead me down a path I never knew I would take. Respite became comfort, comfort became addiction. It happened that fast. I spent the next six years in a same-sex relationship that seemed like utopia to my soul. But it ended badly. Every relationship around me suffered unimaginable damage. My husband, my children, my job, my identity—everything I valued and had cherished imploded.

I wanted to end my life. Depression drove me into a deep, dark hole. But something beautiful happened. Jesus sat with me in that hole.

I didn't find Jesus at church. In fact, church had no idea what to do with me. I may as well have had the plague. Same-sex relationship in church? No one would touch that! So Jesus Himself sat with me. He touched where I hurt. He showed me His own wounds, how He had been abandoned too.

It was a long journey. Together we worked through many years of pain and hurts. But He looked at, held, and listened to each one. And He felt my pain. He cried when I cried. He sweat blood for me. I believe it. It is not just a story to be read. It is a reality.

It is now seven years later. I am finally walking now after attending to that broken leg I so badly wanted acknowledged as a child. It has been quite a process. Deep wounds drive us to desperate realities. My husband stayed with me through it all. My kids too. We have all traversed some rugged valleys, but we are still here, all together.

As for my prior relationship, well, that has transformed as well. We have long gone our separate ways. She also had her own broken leg. Suffice it to say, only He can make all things new again.

I now help others with their unseen pain. I see them walking around with their limps or dragging dead limbs. I stop by the side of the road and help bandage, clean, and repair damage. I let them know they are never alone. Their pain is real. Your pain is real too.

Maybe your pain is abandonment, rejection, or shame. Maybe you know heartache in unimaginably deep ways. Maybe it is a million other things. But whatever it is, Jesus is here. He sees. He knows. He heals.

—Cristi Lorentz, Nevada

BE ENCOURAGED: Jesus sees your pain. He feels your pain, and He will never abandon you. He sits with you in your pain and longs to heal your broken heart. Will you let Him?

Still Alive

I'm really sick," my husband, Adrian, told me. I hurried him to bed. For days, he alternated between bouts of vomiting and diarrhea. One night I made him get up so that I could strip the bed to wash the sheets. I asked if he was feeling better. He shook his head no.

Within the next ninety minutes, I heard a really short cough, and when I checked him, he was having trouble breathing. I called 911. The responders arrived in our area of rural Tennessee in ten minutes. Adrian passed out on the way to the hospital emergency room,

The ER team diagnosed him with Type A influenza and then the following day, double pneumonia. Not long after that he contracted acute respiratory distress syndrome (ARDS), a condition that causes fluid buildup in the lungs. He was rushed to surgery. After I arrived, his physician sat me down and told me, "Your husband is as sick as he can be and still be alive."

Initially, Adrian was put on a prone bed, lying on his stomach, not his back. He was then put on an ECMO (extracorporeal membrane oxygenation) machine. It pumps and oxygenates a patient's blood outside the body.

In all of Memphis, this was the only hospital with an ECMO.

As Adrian lay in the cardiovascular intensive care unit (CVICU), I was told, "Any day someone survives in CVICU is a good day." I spent the day there. My mother had flown in to care for our kids. Later in his stay, I was called in a second time, when I was told that this could be the end for Adrian. With bachelor's and master's degrees in theology and Bible and years of preaching, I was reading my Bible for comfort for myself.

I was about to leave the hospital when a pulmonologist came to talk with me about Adrian. "In the last two weeks your husband has not met even one of the benchmarks we look for," he said. "He's been on double life support (a ventilator and a lung bypass machine). He was in a coma for much of it."

The pulmonologist said that it did not look good, and three options lay before us. The first option was to wait and hope that Adrian's lungs improved. The second option was to give him a lung transplant, but it wasn't a good option since they couldn't transport him to get a lung transplant. With his level of risk, no health facility would accept him. I asked about the third option. Was he going to tell me to pull the plug? "No," he said, "but we have to think of his quality of life."

That evening, I went to a healing service at our church, and people fervently prayed for Adrian. This was around 7:30 p.m. At 10:30 that night, my husband's readings on the monitors suddenly did a 180-degree turn. From that day on, after six weeks of only getting worse, my husband only improved. Within a week, he was removed from the ECMO machine and then weaned off a tracheostomy tube. A week after that, Adrian was sitting up; seven weeks later he was in rehabilitation. He spent six weeks in the ICU, followed by inpatient rehab for seven days. He had to relearn how to walk and use his fine motor skills.

Adrian returned home, and within a week, he was off oxygen. He recovered for less than a month before going back to work. Sickness had gripped my husband for two months, but he was back.

It was a phenomenal medical team that had cared for him. But my best friend's mom was the one who had walked down front in the healing service. She represented the healing that God performed on Adrian over the next few hours. She died the following September. Two weeks before her death, she told me, "I've seen two miracles in my life and Adrian was one of them."

—Sarah Bishop, Tennessee

BE ENCOURAGED: God places a high value on human life. Even as medical professionals work hard to save a loved one whose life hangs in the balance, pray to God, who does all things well. Ask Him for a miracle.

A New Heart

Teal's Story

My husband and I enjoy hiking in the mountains. The thoughts come to me as I'm enjoying nature that had my dad not found faith in God during my childhood, I might not have lived to enjoy these hikes.

My mother pointed our family toward God as she could, but my father really needed to take his role as spiritual leader. We faced hard times. He had skin cancer, and my mother suffered an autoimmune disease. My brother struggled with a wound on his back that wouldn't heal.

My challenge was Raynaud's disease, a malfunctioning in the circulatory system. My body temperature would not regulate. If I got cold, my blood vessels would constrict to keep blood in my core but then not expand afterward. During classes at school, I needed a heater and blanket and wore gloves most of the time.

In desperation, my dad finally reached out for God and began craving the Bible and acquiring a childlike faith in Him. Soon, the Holy Spirit filled my father, who began to manifest a joy he'd never experienced before. As he read his Bible, he also noticed how Jesus healed those who came to Him in faith. As Dad was washing dishes one day, an image of my brother and me came to mind. He asked God why. When God asked him what he wanted most of all, Dad answered that he yearned for his "babies" to be healed. ("Babies," he said, but I was a seventh grader and my brother was a high school junior.)

God told him to read and share with us certain Scripture passages to build our faith. Dad did so and laid hands on my brother and me in prayer. The following morning my brother's wound was healed. I could raise my hands over my head without losing feeling. These were the first of many healings over the next years. Dad's cancer, my mom's autoimmune problem—gone.

As a freshman in high school, I had to take a physical exam to compete in sports. The physician examined my spine, noting that it was curved, possibly as much as a 17 percent curvature. That night Dad laid hands on me and prayed for my spine to become straight. The next day in prayer he heard from God: a second attack would be laid against me. God told him not to be afraid but to stand in faith.

The doctor called—mildly astonished—with no explanation about why the X-rays showed zero percent curvature. And she said to come to her office as soon as possible. We arrived to learn that a shadow had been found on my heart, in addition to two defective arteries. Worst-case scenario? I would die. The best? At least two open-heart surgeries. With success in the surgeries, I would more than likely be in a wheelchair and be limited to short walks.

Shocked, I watched a sports dream fading, but my dad was half giggling as the astonished doctor looked on. "You don't understand, but God already told me this was coming," he said. "So I know its beatable." An echocardiogram would follow.

That night my dad prayed for me again, receiving from God a picture as he prayed. Not a vision, this picture showed Jesus' hands (through his hands) giving me a new heart. With new sports shoes, I played normally in volleyball camp and afterward went for the heart scan. During the ninety-minute drive to the hospital, the enemy tried filling my mind with scenes of me dying or in a wheelchair. Fighting back, I said out loud, "I will not die. My God has given me a new heart!"

My body was scanned, and we were told to await word on surgery dates. Days later, my mother came outside, clutching the phone and shouting. With tears in her eyes, she said the hospital had called. Somehow my heart looked brand-new. I played sports throughout high school, even competing in state volleyball and tennis competitions.

I praise God for giving me a healthy heart, but even more than that, I praise Him for healing the hearts of the people I love. He has poured out His grace on my family and given us new hearts to seek Him and love Him. What an awesome God we serve.

—Teal Donnelly, Iowa

> **BE ENCOURAGED:** An enemy of our souls comes to steal, kill, and destroy, but he is a defeated foe. Jesus was resurrected from the dead, and He advocates for us at the right hand of God the Father. We need to walk in His power over lies.

And Suddenly, There Was Forgiveness

Trieste's Story

Iwas big into running, and most of the races in my area were shorter distances. These races were fun, accessible, and easy for many to enjoy. But personally, I loved running half marathons.

As I ran the streets of my town one early morning, I thought about good friends who were moving overseas to become missionaries. I decided to design and host a half marathon to support their cause. I had no idea where to begin planning such a huge undertaking, but I asked some acquaintances who hosted a yearly 5K race in our town for help getting started.

I quickly made friends with Lisa, the main coordinator of the annual 5K race. We decided to combine forces. We would plan a whole race day, including a half marathon (which I would orchestrate) and a 5K and one-mile fun run, which she would plan as in past years.

We began planning in June, and the race day was set for October. There were many details to work out—some were easy, because they had been worked through before, and others proved challenging. Lisa was encouraging and help-ful. She had a team that had worked with her before, and I recruited my own team of volunteers.

Soon things began to fall apart. Emotions ran high, and different personalities clashed. The people who had planned the 5K in the past had different expectations from the people who were coming in new. Feelings got hurt. Misunderstandings flourished. Expectations were crushed. And by the time our big day rolled around, Lisa and I were hardly speaking. The stress of all the planning and mem-bers of our teams wanting different things made it almost impossible to focus on our relationship. By the time the race was over, the friendship was all but lost. Although we had raised $18,000 for our combined charities, it felt like a loss. My emotions were in the red. And for a long time, it was hard to look back on Race Day with a smile.

Lisa and I avoided each other for some time, which was surprisingly easy even in our smallish town. Then I learned (because it IS a smallish town and word travels fast) that Lisa and her family were moving overseas. "Well," I prayed, "there it all goes. Lord, if You ever want us to reconcile, You're going to have to make it happen in a special way." My wounded heart and I moved on.

Fast-forward about two years. I hadn't spoken with Lisa in all that time, but I had kept tabs on the missionary work she and her family were doing in Haiti. One night I went to a friend's house for a community gathering. I enjoyed these evenings immensely—times of worship, truth from the Word, prayer, and ministry to our hearts and bodies as the Lord led. I often went to these meetings expecting to see God move powerfully in other people's lives, but I didn't expect anything world-changing to happen for me.

About fifty people packed into the large living room, spilling into the kitchen and dining area. I sat on a barstool near the corner and looked around. There, on the other side of the room, was Lisa with her family. I didn't know they were back in the United States.

Before I could decide what to do, Lisa caught my eye. She stood up immediately and started walking my way. I didn't have time to even consider my feelings—whether or not I wanted to see her—but I instantly felt peaceful. She was half-smiling as I stood from my seat. She gave me a tight hug—the kind you don't pull back from for a good minute—and said, "I love you, friend." I said, "I love you too" right back. And in that moment, I knew beyond a shadow of a doubt that reconciliation was taking place. There was no long discussion. No promise of forgiveness. No straightening things out. God just leap-frogged us all the way to the end, where friendship is mended and hearts are healed.

In Acts 16, Paul and Silas were in prison. As they prayed and sang hymns, "suddenly" a violent earthquake shook the jail, opened the doors, and loosed the chains of the prisoners. Paul and Silas were set free. Many times in Scripture God moves suddenly—changing the circumstances of the people involved, shaking everyone's understanding, and releasing them from pain or bondage. That night at my friend's house, Lisa and I experienced the "sudden" presence and healing of God. It was a beautiful moment I'll never forget.

To this day, eight years later, Lisa and I are still friends.

—Trieste Vaillancourt, Oregon

> **BE ENCOURAGED:** Sometime, when you least expect it, God will change your hurt to hope and your heart to healing. Be strong, stay faithful to Him, and expect great things.

Nothing Escapes God's Attention

Bryon's Story

I was getting weaker and weaker, but I did not pay attention to this symptom, nor to my friends' comments about my appearance.

When I finally consulted a physician, I learned that I was suffering from severe anemia, which was caused by Hairy Cell Leukemia (HCL), a rare form of the disease. Admitted to the hospital, I received four pints of blood. It started out being five, but my body had a reaction to the first pint. I remember lying in a hospital and, for the first time, feeling completely helpless in life. Nothing that I could do in and of myself could change the reality of my condition. I had no alternative but to trust God.

I had recently begun pastoring a church, so life was, in a way, just getting started. I was thirty-one years old, and my wife was pregnant with our first child, Elizabeth. HCL requires a one-week treatment with chemotherapy and then a follow-up period to evaluate its effectiveness. If all goes well, the disease can be considered successfully treated within a matter of months.

The assessments of treatment success are done with bone marrow biopsies. Results show whether the chemo has eradicated the leukemia. The night before my second scheduled biopsy, I was looking at my Scripture texts. I was following a Bible in a Year reading plan. Due to this schedule, I just "happened" to be reading Job 21:22–24 NIV: "Can anyone teach knowledge to God, since He judges even the highest? One person dies in full vigor, completely secure and at ease, well nourished in body, bones rich with marrow."

When I read this, I felt that God was *not* proclaiming my healing but was instead telling me that nothing escapes His attention. Not even bone marrow is overlooked. I still carry that with me.

The next day's biopsy results showed that the HCL had been eradicated. It was beautiful to leave the hospital. I had a lot of support. I picked up my baby daughter, Elizabeth, and said, "Now I get to watch you grow up."

The disease returned ten years later. We were in Argentina by then, working as missionaries. I felt myself getting weaker. One gets to know the symptoms of anemia, such as shortness of breath and feeling more tired in exertion. The body's energy is simply depleted.

Just after Christmas, I went for a blood test, which confirmed that the leukemia was back. This time, I was treated in Buenos Aires, so my appointments, tests, results, and consultations with physicians were mostly in Spanish. At times I had difficulty with the new vocabulary. And with three kids during this second time around with HCL, I felt more stressed.

My first medical appointment did not materialize, even though I waited for quite a while. Then after a couple of days, I was called back by another physician. (The facility I had gone to had been short-staffed when I'd been there.) This second doctor told me that she had worked at FundaLeu, a blood disorder hospital in Buenos Aires. She suggested that for better treatment, I go there. So even though the waiting had been inconvenient, the delay in seeing a doctor had worked in my favor. It set in motion a route to better care for me.

Today I am doing well physically, although I do have a hypothyroid condition. My type of leukemia was more treatable, so it was as if I were walking through a door into a world of sickness but stopping just a few feet inside the door, with a good hope of leaving there. Yet in that place were all sorts of afflicted—the old, young people, children, worried parents, dying fathers.

Fear and loneliness were part of the place. It was a heartbreaking gift to see what illness can do to people; it blindsides you and then, if you survive, leaves you changed. But in that place God sustained me by His grace. He even gave me the privilege of leading my hospital roommate to Christ, which was a miracle.

—Bryon Butler, Florida

BE ENCOURAGED: We may be blindsided by illness, even devastated. But our heavenly Father is acutely aware of our needs. He cares about all the details. He can be trusted with every part of our lives.

A Second Chance at Life

Morgan's Story

The Lord spoke to me during a seven-day coma. He gave me a solemn warning that if I didn't turn my life around and look to Him, the disease I was confronting was going to kill me.

Some years before, at sixteen years old, I was diagnosed with an incurable disease known as FSGS (Focal Segmental Glomerulosclerosis), one cause of nephrotic syndrome. My kidneys were functioning at just 20 percent, so my physicians told me that I needed to go on dialysis. Initially, they rejected the idea of a transplant. The disease would cause a buildup of scarring in the new organ in the same way as it had affected my own.

However, because I was on dialysis, I needed a kidney. My Aunt Esta donated a kidney to me. Usually with a kidney transplant, it takes three days for the kidney to function. I was told that the minute mine was hooked up, the kidney started filtering urine and blood.

A checkup two weeks afterward showed that FSGS was invading my new kidney rapidly. It was filling up with scar tissue. Then on New Year's Eve, I began vomiting and became very sick. Once home, I passed out repeatedly and could not even stand up. My live-in boyfriend, Cam, summoned an ambulance.

I was admitted to the University of Michigan Hospital. Already septic—that is, my blood was infected—my kidney had completely stopped working. A part of my heart had failed and half of my liver had failed. When the staff tried to wake me, I attempted to pull out a tube, and so they induced a coma.

During the several days of my coma, Cam didn't leave my side. It was in this period that God spoke to me. When I woke up, Cam said, "We need to get married." We were married within a month of my release from the hospital.

A hemodialysis catheter (or port) inserted during the coma was intended to get my kidneys to start up again. Doctors suggested I would need this procedure for several months, but I thought differently and told them so. "I just really believe that my body's been healed," I said. "You can't be healed from kidney disease," they replied.

I continued with hemodialysis and registered perfect readouts from my kidney during this time. The physicians saw no need for additional procedures. Reiterating that I had been healed, I said, "You guys are going to get this port out next week."

"No," my doctors countered. "We have to keep that in as a precaution." However, the catheter is gone; they removed it. And since then, I have had no kidney problems. The initial scarring of my new kidney never progressed—it just stopped!

Biopsies were taken for two years, showing no new scarring at all. Now, when my blood is drawn, everything is completely normal. It is almost as if I never had kidney disease. The Lord gave me a second chance to live for Him.

I was told I would never be able to carry a child due to the antirejection drugs that I take. But our amazing God allowed me to become pregnant. From the beginning of my pregnancy, medical professionals told me about pre-eclampsia and said that I would spend my pregnancy on bed rest. In spite of scientific documentation of cases like mine, I did not have elevated blood pressure a single time, not even during labor.

I was able to carry our son full term to thirty-eight weeks. At birth, he weighed eight pounds. Since then he has grown into a healthy toddler, with no complications at all. As for me, my kidney function is great, my blood pressure is top-notch, and I have no symptoms of sickness.

I've learned through my suffering and my healing that God is in control and that He wants me to trust Him and live each day for Him—no matter the circumstances. I went from living without paying any attention to God to gratefully seeking Him every day and following Him. I truly was lost and am now found.

—Morgan Powers, Michigan

> **BE ENCOURAGED:** God is long-suffering and His mercy is wide. He is a God who offers us second chances.

Prayers of Deliverance

Heather's Story

I was an eighteen-year-old with a little baby girl and a brand-new marriage to her father that was not working out.

I hung out with users, one of whom advised me with "I have the perfect thing for you." Then he injected me with drugs. For the next three years my life spiraled down to a point as low as ever. Some people may take years to become addicts. In three years, I was doing every drug imaginable. I had needle marks up and down my arms.

In and out of drug rehab, I was homeless. My skin yellow from hepatitis A, I weighed seventy pounds and was fortunate I didn't die. Taking a friend's advice seriously, I left Kansas City to live with my grandmother in southern Texas. I was suffering so badly from detox that for the first week, she had to feed me.

I began going to three Alcoholics Anonymous (AA) meetings a day. When I reached about sixty days of sobriety, I called my old drug dealer, who said he'd bought me a plane ticket back. "All you have to do is go to the airport," he said. So I lied to my grandmother, telling her I was going to Kansas City to spend the weekend with my AA sponsor.

During the thirty-minute drive to the airport, I heard a voice say, "This is the last sixty days you'll ever have." My friend dropped me off, and I went to the ticket counter. I was at the wrong airport! Even in my stupidity God intervened to protect me from myself.

"Are you okay?" a ticket agent asked. "No," I tearfully replied, then began telling her what an awful person I was. She asked where my grandparents lived, saying that I ought to tell them my whole story. Then she fed me and drove me all the way home.

Slowly, steadily came the realization that I could not live a lie, though at this time I hadn't really given my life to the Lord. I worked my way through cosmetology school, where I learned to do manicures. My grandmother drove me to classes because I had lost my driver's license.

I had been clean for a year when I shared my story at the cosmetology school. A woman listening asked me point-blank afterward, "Do you know Jesus? No one just gives up drugs like you did. Your story is incredible."

The truth is that at the age of eleven, I had accepted Jesus as my Savior. However, I hadn't rededicated my life to Him since then. The woman invited me to accompany her to church, where I experienced the presence of God.

I told my new friend that I wanted to be at the church and that I loved Jesus. But I also confided to her that something must be wrong with me because I still wanted to use drugs. She just looked at me as if what I'd said was no big deal and said, "Oh, you just need to be delivered."

"What does that mean?" I asked. "And how do I get it?"

"The next time the pastor asks who needs to be delivered, you run up," she answered. So when that invitation came, I ran to the front. I love a verse from the Bible's New Testament that says, "The prayer of a righteous person is powerful and effective" (James 5:16 NIV).

I witnessed persistent praying in that church that day. Everyone in the church gathered around me and prayed and didn't let go of me until I was free. Whatever had hold of me left my body. It was a radical deliverance. I was different from that day on. The Lord rescued me and healed me.

Since then I've spoken in the same Kansas City rehab facility where I had been a patient. I have told my story—God's story more than my own—for prison ministries and other places as well. I've seen this story hit the hearts of many young women. I've prayed with addicts, and I've been able to help others find freedom in Christ. One thing I know is that He never left me, and because of Him, I'm here today helping to shine His light in dark places.

—Heather Whitworth, Missouri

BE ENCOURAGED: We find it easy to think that we have sunk too low for God's hand to reach us, but it is just not true. Around the world God is rescuing people every day from their bad decisions and addictions. Their stories may differ, but He is the same to each and every one. He is the Savior.

When God Takes the Place of an Obsession

Emily's Story

At a buffet-style restaurant, when I was nine years old, I ate nine pieces of pizza. Why? It was my older brother's dare. He said, "Hey, you want to challenge our friends to see who can eat the most pizza?" and I wanted to be cool. I did it. I don't remember exactly who scarfed down the most pizza.

So began a couple of habits with me. One, I would compete with my brother. And two, this competition didn't stop at mealtimes. I would want as much food or more than he had whenever we sat down to a meal. I would feel full—stuffed even—but not to the point of feeling nauseated or needing to vomit.

By the eighth grade, I was running with the cross-country team and playing basketball and volleyball at my school. Extremely active, I did not gain weight despite all the eating. I would always work it off. "Everything's okay," I told myself. "I'll just cut back when I quit sports." Reflecting back on those days, however, I now would say that I struggled with gluttony.

My lifestyle continued this way throughout high school and college—an unhealthy attitude about eating, which was masqueraded by my heavy involvement in sports. To look at me, one wouldn't see a problem. But inside, I knew better.

I received a college scholarship for cross-country. Studying nursing, I was taking some nutrition classes. In the first of these, the professor told us to manage and track everything we were eating. *Oh, I don't need to do that,* I thought, with my pride rising up. *I'm an athlete. I run five miles a day. I need to be able to eat.*

The assignment—and those of other nutrition courses—planted a notion in me that I ought to consume foods that are nutritious and abstain from some things. However, it remained for me at the time simply a notion, an idea. My athleticism continued as my rationale for continuing to consume an unhealthy balance of food. *You need to have enough energy,* a voice in my mind said. *You need to eat and eat and eat.*

When full, my stomach gave faulty messaging to my brain. I just kept eating. Another faulty message would also settle in my mind: I had to finish the food on my plate. Or I'd tell myself, *You paid for that; you should eat it.*

After graduating from college, I addressed the overeating problem and said, "Okay, you really need to control this." I'd had nutrition courses, but I felt that I didn't know enough about the topic to help myself. I did not know what to do. So at this point, I prayed, "God, help me stop eating so much. I can't stop." That prayer seemed to trigger a realization: "I can't stop."

Earlier my struggle wasn't visible, but now my weight began to tell the real story. Office work did not offer much exercise. I gained thirty pounds in several months. Some of my problem lay in my choices of foods, but the bigger issue was plate cleaning.

A slow process of change began for me around the age of twenty-one. I accepted my sister's invitation to attend a nondenominational church. The congregation held services throughout the weekend: Friday, Saturday, and Sunday. I found these services very different from what I had grown up with—they were much livelier.

Over time, I developed a stronger relationship with God. I began to understand that He is for me, not against me. My moments of begging God and pleading for help stopped. In their place I felt comfort knowing that He wants to help me in all of life, not just during a pinch. Through intimacy with the Lord, I began changing my eating habits. Soon enough I was taking food home from the big portions served in restaurants. I started working out with a personal trainer at a gym. Eventually the voices about food and finishing my plate were silenced. I lost fifty pounds, got married, had three kids, and no longer have an obsession with food.

During the time God walked me through my obsession with food, He was revealing different parts of my life that needed to be changed. Overeating was just one area where He slowly worked in me. I've found that God wants to change all of me so I can follow Him with my whole being—my heart, my mind, and my body. Because of the work He's accomplished in my life, I can encourage other people to trust Him to work life-changing healing in their lives too.

—Emily Bryan, Kansas

BE ENCOURAGED: Admitting that we have a problem is a first step to overcoming it. Declaring our dependence on God is another critical step. God waits to strengthen us in our weakness.

Over the Jordan

Marqus's Story

At the age of three, I was diagnosed with sickle cell hemoglobin disease (similar to sickle cell anemia). The disease affected my hemoglobin, causing my white blood count to drop.

I had my first sickle cell crisis as a teen, a time of excruciating pain in my knees and elbows. Later in college in Louisiana, one such episode sent me to the infirmary. When I returned home, a major sickle cell crisis landed me in the hospital. Contracting pneumonia, I also got acute chest syndrome, which collapses the lungs and makes breathing very difficult. A bolus fentanyl for pain relief prompted an allergic reaction, and I needed help to begin breathing again.

That night I recalled my mentor's story of God twice answering her pleas to save her life. He let her know that she might not get a third chance. When I heard God say to me in that hospital, "Surrender now," that's what I did. I gave my life to Christ. I had not done this before, even though I had attended church as a child.

The next two years brought nine more hospital visits. During a six-week stay in the hospital, I rejected the medical specialists' plans to give me a bone marrow transplant. The body's immune system is compromised in this procedure, requiring patient quarantine. I didn't want to be quarantined and did not have a transplant.

A member of my church congregation came to me one Sunday, saying, "God wants to heal you, but you need to have faith." I went home and began praying earnestly. A month later, she invited me to her house, along with some other church ladies. As I crossed her threshold, I remembered a verse from the Old Testament book of Isaiah: "I saw the Lord, high and exalted, seated on a throne; and the train of His robe filled the temple" (6:1 NIV). I felt God's presence as I entered the house. I began worshipping, crying, and praying.

"Marqus, sit down on this chair, and we're going to pray over you," a lady said. "We're going to lay our hands on you and ask God to heal you." When I got up afterward, I took a step and almost fell.

"I feel so light," I said.

A woman said of the sickness, "It's not on you anymore. You've been healed."

"I wholeheartedly believe it," I replied. "I am healed." As we started singing hymns and rejoicing, I remember thinking, "I don't have to deal with sickle cell anymore." Later, as we read in the Old Testament about Joshua leading the people of Israel across the Jordan River into the Promised Land, I felt as though God were ferrying me over my own Jordan.

Not long after my healing experience, I was experiencing pain in my knee and made an appointment to see my doctor. At the appointment, he was convinced sickle cell pain had brought me in. "No, it's not sickle cell," I said. "I've been healed." The doctor dismissed the answer.

We learned that an infection had gotten into my knee, but as he looked at the laboratory results of my blood test, he kept asking, "Are you sure that you had sickle cell?"

"Why do you ask that?" I replied.

"Your hemoglobin level is perfect; your white blood count is perfect," he answered. "Everything is perfect, and this is never the case when someone has sickle cell." He left and another doctor entered. "Are you *sure* you have had sickle cell?" he asked. Same scenario as the last one. Even though my doctor—who is a believer—had advised me to get my blood tested regularly as a precaution, I was eventually told that I didn't need to return for blood tests for the rest of my life.

Like the Israelites, who memorialized the day God brought them into the Promised Land with twelve stones they had taken from the middle of the Jordan River, I wanted to set up a memorial as a reminder of God's healing in my life. I grew my hair long and put it in dreadlocks. My dreads commemorate the day that God healed me. Since my healing, I have continued to pursue a deeper understanding of God. I became a minister, and I have the privilege and joy of reaching out to people with love, teaching them God's Word, and witnessing God's healing in their lives.

—Marqus Rose, Missouri

BE ENCOURAGED: Our God is the great Deliverer and Healer. He guides us and provides a way for us to cross over into newness of life.

A Journey from Despair to Hope

Vince's Story

The journey my wife, Rose, and I have been on, like so many, has had its high and low points. We had been Christians for twenty years and were into our thirteenth year of pastoring when we were faced with a crisis. Even while preaching and teaching at least four times a week, I found myself suicidal and wanting to leave my wife and four sons to run away somewhere and hide. On top of that, I was angry, controlling, and way too authoritative in my role as pastor. I probably hurt more people than I helped during that time.

At this same time, Rose was dealing with deafening thoughts of failure, not being good enough, and wondering where the abundant life was that the apostle John talked about. Like many Christians, we had been in the church long enough to be able to preach and teach on God's love, but we honestly felt His love was conditional, selective, and performance based.

I was so overly strict and demanding on my boys that apart from the grace of God, I might have lost them to the enemy. My actions at home toward them did not reflect the love of God the Father that I preached every week.

Rose and I had been married for more than twenty-three years, and while I loved her, I was never able to fully open my heart to her. I sheltered myself behind a wall of protection and privacy. I had become a good actor by developing the ability to identify and portray someone I was not.

We found ourselves trying to earn a love that could not be earned. We were attempting to impress a God who had already, since before the foundation of the world, determined that we were worth everything. He had freely given us His love by sending His Son, Jesus, to die for us, yet we just did not understand that His gift to us included not only Christ's death to suffer the punishment for our sins but also Jesus' continued presence in our lives. We weren't allowing Jesus to live in and through us in covenant relationship.

Rose and I carried so much baggage from our childhoods into our marriage. The brokenness and disappointments from our pasts were defining our present. The lies we had believed about ourselves and the cracks in our foundations those lies created became the set of glasses by which we viewed ourselves, other people, and God Himself.

In our brokenness, God brought to our attention our need for His love and acceptance to permeate every aspect and relationship of our lives. There was work to do. Rose and I started this journey by forgiving the people in our pasts who had helped create a paradigm in us that led to an endless road of hopelessness, despair, and frustration. We examined our own lives and repented of our participation in and partnership with the condemning lies we had believed about ourselves. Through this, we discovered something we had desperately needed all along the way— each other. We worked to help and support each other in accepting God's love for ourselves and for each other. We no longer needed to work separately through our struggles and our pain. As husband and wife, allied together, we moved forward into God's love.

Then, when our eyes began to open and healing started coming, we began to see what had been there the whole time—a loving heavenly Father who was calling us to Himself. When this healing process began unfolding for us, the Bible became more real to us than ever before. Suddenly, we read Scripture from a whole different perspective. Genuine, not forced, love came upon us through God's Word, and that love flowed out of us to each other, our children, and even toward ourselves.

We have come so far in this journey, but we are reminded that the journey does not stop until we are face-to-face with our heavenly Father. Rose and I now have the tools to support each other when needed and to garden our own hearts rather than depending on others to do it for us.

Getting God's love from our heads to our hearts has been the result of this journey. We are seeing more and more what He really thinks of us and that as sons and daughters of God, we have Jesus Himself living not only in us but through us! We have found healing from the brokenness of our past and healing and life in Christ.

—Vince Mercardante, Georgia

BE ENCOURAGED: God isn't waiting for you to impress Him or become perfect before He'll love and accept you. He has already loved you and accepted you. That's why He willingly sent His Son, Jesus, to die for you! He's waiting for you to accept His love and share that love with the people around you.

He Heals Our Deepest Hurts

Charity's Story

My husband, a pilot, had arrived home from a mission and was acting strangely. When I asked him what was wrong, he replied, "I just don't want to do this anymore."

"You can change jobs," I said. "We can do whatever you need."

His answer caught me completely off guard: "I don't want to be married anymore."

After his next mission, he returned home and handed me divorce papers. Just three months earlier, we'd become the parents of a son, Joshua. My heart shattered. Fearful at first, I later turned inward and shut down emotionally.

Almost immediately after the divorce papers were filed, our assets were frozen. I had no money. My husband planned to sell my horse, trailer, and truck, so I put those things into hiding. After teaching one last dog training class, I had no way to support myself and our son.

Amid bewildering chaos, a miracle happened. "My husband and I felt like we needed to give you this," my neighbor said, handing me three hundred dollars. A couple from my church congregation let Joshua and me live in their house while they went on a mission trip. I told my trainer that I'd be selling my horse. She said that I absolutely could not and that she'd care for him until I had access to funds again.

God was taking care of every detail for us—and it was a good thing, for I was flagging under enormous pressures. I could not function enough to bring myself to appear in court to finalize the divorce. When my husband was dispatched overseas, we were still married.

My mother arrived and helped me find a rental in the middle of nowhere—Noodle, Texas. The homeowner compassionately lowered the rent for us. I worked at a church and continued training dogs. I was able to have Joshua with me and not pay to put him in daycare. At the food pantries, I found diapers, formula, and baby wipes for Joshua on every visit. God provided it *all*. Even though I had very little money, I remembered always to tithe—to give a tenth of my income to God's work.

I needed to continue paying a mortgage on our New Jersey house, where my mother-in-law lived. She refused to leave. I hired an attorney, asking him, "Can I pay once I've sold the house?" He agreed and began to take care of the eviction. Meanwhile, my divorce lawyer repeatedly "forgot" to send me invoices.

At a spiritual conference I attended in Kansas City, people formed a tunnel and prayed for me as I walked between them. The experience became the beginning of a long healing process in my heart.

Later another Kansas City congregation caught my attention, and I decided to visit the church and attend its weekend worship services. My mother and I traveled to the Kansas City metro area in separate vehicles (I wanted time alone to think and pray). Throughout the weekend services, I felt nothing. However, a woman named Kay came over to me. "You know," she said, "people move here."

Driving back to Texas, I couldn't help but think I had left something valuable, like my wallet, back at the church. Thinking about this led me into a panic attack—the worst I have ever experienced. I yelled at God, "What? Are You trying to tell me to move to Kansas City?"

I called the Texas church where I worked, and the lady who answered sobbed to me that the pastor was leaving. "Well," I blurted out, "I'm leaving too." I pulled off the road, and my mom pulled off too. Hearing my plans, she exclaimed, "I knew it! I told God He would need to tell you because you wouldn't listen to me."

The day I packed up in Texas, my brother called from New Jersey to say that my mother-in-law was moving from my house. Within a week, it sold—to a buyer willing to pay cash. I finally had money and a new start at life in Kansas City. I first worked as a horse trainer and soon got a job with a more reliable paycheck.

The pastor of my new church said, "You give us six months. Listen and apply the teaching; you won't know yourself." I stayed six months, and for each month I stayed, a layer of past hurts would fall away. Sometimes growth was a slow process. Other times it was like a bolt of lightning.

God restores! I went from being a heartbroken woman with no path, no money, no car, no house to a thriving, strong individual who is standing on His promises every single day.

—Charity Willison, Texas

> **BE ENCOURAGED:** Our loving heavenly Father places people and circumstances in our lives that help us move closer to Him and to the plans He has in store for us.

LIVE YOUR FAITH

Dear Friend,

This book was prayerfully crafted with you, the reader, in mind—every word, every sentence, every page—was thoughtfully written, designed, and packaged to encourage you...right where you are this very moment. At DaySpring, our vision is to see every person experience the life-changing message of God's love. So, as we worked through rough drafts, design changes, edits and details, we prayed for you to deeply experience His unfailing love, indescribable peace, and pure joy. It is our sincere hope that through these Truth-filled pages your heart will be blessed, knowing that God cares about you—your desires and disappointments, your challenges and dreams.

He knows. He cares. He loves you unconditionally.

BLESSINGS!
THE DAYSPRING BOOK TEAM

Additional copies of this book and other DaySpring titles can be purchased at fine retailers everywhere.
Order online at dayspring.com
or
by phone at 1-877-751-4347